A Light to All Japan

The Story of Susan Dyck

Eugene Neudorf

Christian Publications, Inc.
Camp Hill, Pennsylvania

Christian Publications, Inc.
3825 Hartzdale Drive, Camp Hill, PA 17011
www.cpi-horizon.com

Faithful, biblical publishing since 1883

ISBN: 0-87509-724-3
LOC Catalog Card No.: 97-77647

Cover portrait by Karl Foster

Dedication

To the readers of this story—

we need more Susans in the Church today
who will respond to the call of God
upon their lives
to go where He asks them to go;
who will develop a burning desire
to reach the lost;
who will have the courage to attempt
things for God
that all but Him consider impossible;
who will give more sacrificially;
who will pray more fervently;
who will allow their children to go.

To the young men and women
of this generation—

who will be part of a spiritual uprising
so that when God asks, "Who will go?"
they will respond with the words,
"Send me, Lord! I am Yours!"

Contents

Acknowledgments

In the early '80s I heard Susan give her testimony on a Sunday evening at the Alliance Church in Prince Albert, Saskatchewan. As she spoke, one overwhelming thought consumed me. This was a story that needed telling! Little did I think that I would be the person telling it. It has been an honor to do so.

It's also been a long time in coming. There were times when I wondered if I would ever complete it, or even if I was worthy to write the story. But, finally, after a career change, seminary, ordination, pastoring in two different churches—and some periods of procrastination—the book is finished. However, without the help of a number of people, it would not have become a reality. My thanks goes to:

Bernie Palmer for giving me the confidence to tackle this project and for giving me direction in the early going. I admire him greatly as a friend and author.

Betty Dyck, Susan's sister, for the many hours she spent going over the manuscript ensuring that things were accurate. She has been a real encouragement to me throughout the process.

Randy and Regan, my sons, who encouraged me to keep plugging away, nudged me to start again when I laid the project aside for a time and prayed for me on countless occasions. Any father would be proud to call them his sons.

Rhona, my loving wife, partner and best friend, who painstakingly edited each chapter for me and through her insight added much to the story. I also thank her for her patience and gentleness, for her willingness to keep suggesting changes even when I wasn't ready to immediately accept them. Because of her I am a better writer, a better friend, father and husband.

Susan, a remarkable woman who defied the odds, an exemplary missionary whose love for the Japanese people knew no boundaries, a deeply devoted Christian saint who truly believed that nothing was impossible with God. I thank her for allowing me to tell her incredible story, for teaching me what it means to be a person of faith, for reminding me that we can know God intimately with every fiber of our being.

And finally, my *Heavenly Father*, for being my Savior and Lord, for giving me a passion and a desire to write, for guiding me through each chapter. Through Susan, He taught me what it means to live a Christlike life.

Editor's Note

Because this book was compiled from information provided by Susan's sister Betty and from interviews with and letters written by Susan, Mr. Neudorf has told the story in first person—as if from the mouth of Susan herself. Certain dialogue has been recreated.

1

Fear and Fire

Staring out the side window of the car, I watched the white line defining the shoulder of the highway flash by and the long grass and endless string of fence posts blur into the gray horizon. Although the chill of early spring was still in the air, I knew it would be only a matter of time before the wide expanse of the prairie burst forth with every color imaginable.

Winters on the prairies are extremely cold and long, and one can't help but appreciate the changing of the seasons—that first tree bud as it reveals its beauty to the world, that first new blade of grass as it pushes up from the earth that spawned it, that first flower, the humble crocus, as its blooms unfold in understated modesty.

Having left Saskatoon twenty minutes earlier, I couldn't help but wonder at the excitement that was starting to build inside me. Finally, as we turned off the main highway and headed west, the countryside began to look increasingly familiar. I recognized a farmhouse where I had worked more than forty years earlier. Leaning forward, I gazed intently through the windshield, searching for the first glimpse of the Aberdeen elevators against the prairie skyline. I didn't have to wait long. Memories once forgotten flooded my mind as though I was being transported back in time.

It seemed like only yesterday that my life had begun in the rural community surrounding this quaint and quiet little town in central Saskatchewan, Canada. Although nothing special to a stranger passing by, to me the sight of Aberdeen represented twenty years of my life.

Leaving the highway, we jolted across the railway tracks and headed down the main street. On one side of this short, quiet avenue stood the elevators and train station. Lining the other side were the gas station, general store and assorted little shops that make up a typical rural Saskatchewan community.

The Empress Hotel, a red-brick, two-story building, looked a little more time-worn than I remembered it, but still as sturdy as ever. It had seen its share of changes. The third floor was gone now; some of the windows on the remaining two had been bricked in; others had been replaced.

We parked in front of the hotel and walked

inside. It was hardly recognizable, but the memories could not escape me. I had worked there and lived in a tiny room on the now de-molished third floor. I thought back to the day when, in that very room, my life changed direc-tion, the day when I . . . but I'm getting ahead of myself.

Climbing back into the car, we crossed the railway tracks once more. We hadn't traveled far when Betty asked the driver to slow down. She pointed out the land where our charming yet efficient one-room schoolhouse had flour-ished. A brand new house now stood where the school used to be, but that did nothing to stop the memories. I recalled the big, old, pot-bel-lied stove, warm and inviting as we came in out of the cold, dark winter mornings. I heard again the sound of the horses breaking trail and the steel runners of the sleigh cutting into the crisp virgin snow. I smiled as I caught the harmony of children's voices cutting through the biting air, greeting friends at the end of a long and chilly ride. . . .

Numerous rocks dotted the roadside. I ex-plained to the driver how the first settlers be-gan clearing the land, moving the larger rocks to make it suitable for farming. Eventually, they ended up near the roadside where some of the deeply religious Mennonite pioneers painted Bible verses on them. As a little girl, I walked to school passing those rocks every day. Unfortunately, at that time, a Bible verse was

simply a superstitious saying to be recited
when passing the graveyard at Clarkboro.

As we neared an intersection Betty instructed
the driver to turn right. There was that very
graveyard, now overgrown with weeds. On the
other side of the road, beyond the tracks, stood
a few granaries with a small, winding trail leading to them. It was all that remained of the
once neat little village of Clarkboro.

A tear came to my eye as I thought of the
"dressed up" village it used to be and of the
train that I boarded there so many years ago, a
train that took me to a destination I could
never in my wildest dreams have imagined.

"How close are we to your Grandma's farm?"
our driver asked.

"It's just over the next hill," Betty replied.

Happy memories began to swell within me as
we neared the crest of the hill. Not only had
we visited Grandma's farm many times as children—it eventually became our home.

But as we topped the hill my heart dropped.
The once beautiful farm nestled in the little valley just off the grid road was no more. Suddenly,
I was taken back, back fifty years. I no longer
saw the run-down condition of the farm, the
gray, weather-beaten, two-story house that had
long since fallen down or the weeds in the garden and the grass that had gone wild. No! What
I envisioned was a lovely home with a colorful
yard and verdant garden whose elegance and
grandeur could only be compared to . . .

We turned in at the driveway and pulled up in front of what used to be the farm house.

"It's too bad no one lives here, Susan," my sister sighed as we got out of the car.

"Yes," I replied wistfully. "It would have been nice to be able to see everything the way it used to be." I paused for a moment. "Especially the garden. I really miss the garden!"

We walked around the yard picking our way gingerly through the rubble and pondering how things used to be.

"You know, Susan," Betty interjected, "it seems only a short while since Mom and Dad lived here."

"I know, Betty," I replied. "Things sure fell apart quickly with no one caring for the place."

We climbed back into the car and directed the driver to a homestead which, although not my birthplace, happened to be the first one I could recall. As we drove, the earliest years of my life started to flow through my brain like movies on a giant screen. In actuality, only a barren hill was all that remained of the site where I had spent my childhood years. On the right, in the valley below, between the road and the South Saskatchewan River, was the land we had farmed. It was here that the first of many tragedies befell our family. However, my story did not begin there. Rather, it began under very ordinary circumstances one winter's day.

On March 7, 1922, in a little farmhouse in rural Saskatchewan, not far from the village of Edinberg, Henry and Susan Dyck gave birth to a daughter. The fourth of nine children, they named me after my mother.

Mom was a soft-spoken, gentle woman; my father, a big man of stark contrasts. His kindness and care were demonstrated in many ways. He loved children, was very hospitable and was always ready to lend a helping hand to someone in need. He often sang the old church hymns, even shedding a tear now and then.

Conversely, when his temper got the better of him, he could be very unreasonable, especially when it came to disciplining his children. He certainly would tolerate no "back talk," nor would he allow his authority to be questioned even if he happened to be in the wrong. As time went by, he also developed a weekend drinking problem. During those times his rage would become uncontrollable, a fearful thing to behold, especially for a vulnerable child.

My father was a carpenter by trade. Although very good at what he did, he found it hard to feed a growing family on a carpenter's wage alone. Bill, the oldest child, was born in 1916, followed by John, Tena, myself, Nick, Helen, Annie, Henry and Betty—all within fifteen years. After the first five children, Dad decided it was time to find a larger house and an extra source of income. The most obvious choice was to buy a farm.

After a brief search, Dad found a suitable place one mile west of his parents' place. There, on a hill overlooking the fields and the South Saskatchewan River, he remodeled a modest two-story building. Although still cramped for space, we were better off than before and no worse off than most families in the area.

In 1929, the Great Depression hit. By then, Dad had begun drinking heavily every second weekend. For the most part though, he and Mom were able to hide it from us kids. But it wouldn't be long until things would change for the worse.

Our family knew very little about the Bible or of Jesus Christ and the sacrifice He had made for us on the cross. The only Bible we had was an old German one with lots of pictures. Unfortunately it was seldom opened and I never learned to read German. So what little I did learn came from those pictures.

Mom and Dad tried to tell us what they knew about the Bible, but the information was often distorted. As a result, I developed an unhealthy fear of certain things. In fact, the fear of death I experienced around graveyards no doubt came from something my mother told me.

One day I came running into the house.

"Mom, Mom!" I screamed in terror, slamming the door behind me.

"What is it, Susan?" she asked.

"Mom! C-c-can we ever know i-i-if we're g-g-going to go to heaven?" I stammered, gasping for breath. I have no idea what prompted the question, but I anxiously waited for what I hoped would be a favorable answer.

After a brief pause my mother replied, "Child, I wish there was a way to know, but it's just not so. Not until our deathbed do we know whether we're going to heaven or not."

My heart fell! A numbness settled into my soul, a sense of despair that did not go away for a very long time. She finished off our little talk by giving me a verse from the Bible that I'm sure she thought would bring me comfort. The next time I walked past the Clarkboro graveyard on my way to school, I blurted out, "Be merciful to me a sinner!" Those words became for me an oft-repeated incantation rather than a cry to God for forgiveness. And, when I could, I skirted the graveyard altogether.

Although the Depression and drought was relentlessly beginning to take its toll, we were able to get a harvest in the year I turned nine. However, later that fall, tragedy struck.

It began like any other day around harvesttime. Long before dawn, Dad got up, ate the breakfast Mom had waiting for him, hitched the horses to the binder and made his way to the field in the valley below.

John and Tena went off to school; Bill and I were sent into town to get some medicine and the five younger children stayed at home. Of the ones left behind, Nick was the oldest—he had just turned eight. Betty, the youngest, was still an infant.

Shortly after lunch, Mom went down to the field where Dad was working. One of the turkeys had strayed from the farm and laid her eggs in the field. Dad had asked Mom to come and show him where they were so the nest would not be disturbed.

While she was gone, the house suddenly caught on fire. By the time Dad happened to look up, smoke was billowing from the windows and flames were hungrily licking at the wooden frame. Dad broke into a frantic run, charging up the hill.

"Oh, God! Please save my children!" he shouted in anguish, unaware that eight-year-old Nick had decided to take them for a walk. Needless to say, Dad was incredibly relieved when everyone turned out to be safe.

By the time the rest of us returned, there wasn't much left of the house. Dad and the two older boys continued to watch over the smoking embers throughout the afternoon so the fire wouldn't spread. Some of us helped Mom retrieve the horses and hitch them to the wagon. The rest of us piled in for the ride to Grandma's place just down the road. By the time we arrived at her house it was already

dark. But it was a long time before any of us
felt like sleeping.

The cause of the fire? That question was
never answered to our satisfaction.

The next morning we climbed into the wagon
once again, this time to make our way back to
the farm. Dad was very quiet, hardly noticing
the chatter going on around him.

By the time we reached the farm, only two
sounds could be heard—the snorting of the
horses and the creaking of the wagon as it
bounced over the rutted trail.

We gazed in stony silence at the sight before
us. A few charred, black timbers were all that
remained erect of our once beautiful but modest little home. Some of the timbers had fallen
in a crisscross pattern, as though leaning on
each other for support. All in all they presented
a brooding contrast against the pale blue sky. A
tremendous feeling of loneliness came over
us—a Mom and Dad and nine children in an
old farm wagon. The stark reality of what had
happened was almost too much for us to bear
at that moment, especially for Dad.

Everything was hopelessly ruined! Nothing
was salvageable! Except for the clothes on our
backs, we had lost it all. As if in a daze we silently picked through the ashes. But we found
only a couple of black, sooty, misshapen, metal
pots. As the day drew to a close, it was truly an
exhausted, disheartened and dirty family that
made its way back to Grandma's house.

The next few months dragged by. Neighbors helped out as much as they could, but times were rough for everyone. We moved into what had once been a grainery on Grandma's yard. Because it wasn't winterized, it became imperative that Dad search for more adequate housing before the frost came. He finally decided to renovate another old house located on the same property.

In the meantime, for most of us, things slowly began to get back to normal. But for Dad, life did not get any better. Before the fire, he drank heavily, mostly on weekends and then only at night when all of us were asleep. After the fire, however, there were times when he came home while we were still awake. Mom would shoo us up to bed as quickly as possible, where, as his temper raged, I would cower in fright under the covers.

Now don't get me wrong. Whenever Dad lost his temper in front of the children, he was quick to apologize the next morning after he had sobered up. But to a nine-year-old girl, those bouts of anger could be a scary thing. In fact, it was on one of those occasions that I actually feared for my life.

2

The Escape

I began to spend a great deal of time at
Grandma's place, especially in the garden
adjacent to her house. It became my favorite spot to visit, particularly when I was troubled about something. I don't know why it had
such an effect on me. There just happened to
be something wonderful about standing in the
middle of that beautiful oasis and escaping my
troubles at least temporarily. I revisited that
spot in my mind many times over the years,
visualizing with amazing clarity the serenity
and simplicity of Grandma's garden. Things
were far from nice during the Depression, but
even during the worst of times Grandma's yard
seemed to express the fact that somebody
cared.

For most people, a garden out front would
have been plenty. But not for my grandmother.
Her "real" garden was on the far side of the

house surrounded by trees. Nestled among those trees was Grandma's well. It held the coolest, clearest and most refreshing water I ever tasted. After spending time munching on Grandma's delectables, we would often go down to the well, sit in the shade created by the magnificent maples and quench our thirst.

Anyway, Grandma's garden was the place I used to go when I felt frightened or threatened, at least when the weather permitted. Other times, my bed had to suffice. What I'm about to tell you has to do with my father. It's not pleasant, but I believe he would want it to be told so that other fathers could learn from his mistakes.

As the Depression and drought dragged on in the prairies, farming became increasingly more difficult and jobs scarce. The fact that Dad couldn't provide for us began to weigh heavily on his mind. As a result, he became depressed at times, and that depression caused him to drink even more heavily.

Now, when my father drank, he became a different person, moody and angry. His anger would often be expressed in foul language accompanied by the threat of physical violence either toward us or himself. However, he never threatened Mother.

During one of his drinking bouts he came in from outside and shouted, "Get me a knife, Mom! Or, better still, make it a gun!"

Mom, who always waited up for him when he

went drinking, herded us up to bed and then
quietly asked, "Why, Henry?"
"I'm going to kill the children and then do
away with myself. That's why!" he answered in
a slurred voice. "It's the only way to end our
problems." Whether Dad would ever have done
such a thing, I don't really know. I seriously
doubt it now. But to a young girl of ten with a
healthy imagination, those were terrifying experiences. Thankfully, Mom usually was able to
calm him down until he either forgot about his
threats or mercifully fell into a deep sleep.

During a bitterly cold and windy winter
night, I was witness to another frightening incident. It was getting late and Dad was still not
home. Mom kept interrupting her mending,
glancing from time to time at the clock on the
wall. When it struck nine she finally called Bill
and asked him to go out and find his father.

After he left, everyone got very quiet. All we
could do was sit and wait, each with his or her
own thoughts, contemplating what Bill might
find. It seemed like an eternity had passed
when we finally heard a car drive up. Suddenly
the front door pushed open and in came Bill,
staggering under the weight of my father. He
pushed away from Bill and let out a stream of
oaths that made our ears burn.

"Hurry children," Mom said, pointing directly at us. "Go upstairs and get to bed."

I was the last one up. As I reached the top
stair, I looked back. Dad was still teetering

back and forth in the middle of the room, with Mom, Bill and John watching him. I ran to my bed as fast as I could and hid under the covers. It didn't help alleviate my fears though. The walls were like paper, and no matter how hard I tried not to, I heard every word.

For the next minute or so Dad continued to curse at no one in particular. Then suddenly, in mid-sentence, he stopped. His eyes rolled up and he fell backward, crashing to the floor. Bill, thinking Dad was about to die, dropped down on top of him. The last thing I remember hearing before I fell into a troubled sleep was Bill crying out, "Oh, God! Oh, God! Please save him!"

That night Dad came very close to drinking himself to death. Thankfully he didn't. A few nights later, on Christmas day, he once again apologized for his conduct and once again things were back to normal, at least for a while, until the next time.

It was one morning in the late spring or early summer. Dad had come into the house before lunch, already fairly intoxicated. Whether he had gone into town early that morning or had brought some alcohol home the night before, I never was able to determine. In any case, I could see that he had been drinking, although it was obvious that he still had most of his senses about him.

Dad was a big, strong man and when he got mad I felt as if he were towering over me. He began shouting at Mother. The more I looked at him, the more I thought he might hit me.

Suddenly, with a shriek of terror, I ran out of the house, crying uncontrollably. Hardly able to see where I was going, I stumbled my way across the driveway and through the grass. It didn't matter that I could barely see because of the tears—I could have found my way blind-folded to my destination, Grandma's garden. I had come to escape, to find release from my fears.

I don't know what caused me to do what I did next, but suddenly I looked up into the sky, beyond the fluffy white clouds and into the brilliant blue expanse. With tears still pouring down my face and in a fearful quaking voice I cried out, "God, God! I know You are up there! Up there way beyond those clouds and blue sky. If You will protect me now, when I grow up, I will serve You." I was only ten years old, but already I felt like I had lived a lifetime.

As the months went by I forgot about that desperate prayer in Grandma's Eden. In fact, none of us had too many thoughts about God. Once in awhile, at Mom's suggestion, we would go to an all-German church, but I couldn't understand it. When I was fifteen, for a brief time Dad too became somewhat inter-ested in attending church. But once again, be-cause of the German-only services, I soon became disinterested.

The effects of the Depression became increasingly more palpable with every passing year. Each summer that followed the preceding one seemed to get hotter and drier. There was hardly enough moisture to grow anything. Oh, the winters gave us relief from the heat, and the snow that fell brought some initial moisture during the spring thaw, but when the rains failed to materialize it wasn't long before the crops dried up and the prairie winds blew the topsoil away, depositing it into the ditches along the roads.

Then, in 1935, during the height of the Depression, Mother took sick. For an entire year I stayed home as she slowly recuperated from an illness that was never diagnosed. I was thirteen years old. Following that, I completed grade five and then had to drop out of school to help support the household.

A great many responsibilities were heaped upon my shoulders and during the following four years I worked as a hired girl on a dairy farm and as a live-in maid at a wealthy landowner's acreage. Most of the money went home to Mom and Dad.

In 1941, two years after the war broke out, I found a new job. It was to lead me into a new life, a life I never knew existed. Even though God was primarily a stranger to our family during those years, I was about to find out that He had not forgotten us.

3

A Lump of Clay

It was the spring of '41. Fearful and lonely, a disillusioned young woman, I took a job as a waitress at the Empress Hotel in Aberdeen, hoping desperately that the change would add some spark to my life. But the two years in Aberdeen simply magnified my inner turmoil. I couldn't explain it—I had a good job, friends and a community with which I was familiar. I knew that everyone had to deal with some level of depression from time to time, but I also knew that usually they were able to overcome it or at least cope with it to some degree. But as the months dragged on, the tension within me increased and intensified until no solution seemed possible. Then, in January of 1943, during a cold and windy week just prior to my twenty-first birthday, something happened that changed the course of my life forever.

It all started when two local businessmen and their wives—the Schroeders and the Regiers—invited the Reverend Ed Erickson, an evangelist, to speak for a week in our town hall. Bill and Katherine Schroeder owned the local hardware store and Abe Regier ran one of the elevators in town. Little did I know the impact these couples would have on my life.

A woman who knew my mother approached me one day early that week.

"Susan," she said. "I'm concerned for you. You used to be such a happy little girl when you were growing up. Now your eyes show nothing but sadness. What's wrong?"

"I don't know," I stammered shyly, looking down at my feet. Then suddenly the floodgates burst open.

"I just don't feel like being happy!" I blurted. "There's nothing to be happy about!"

"Well, young lady," she replied ever so softly, "I'm not sure if this is going to help, but you've heard about the special meetings at our town hall?" I nodded. "Well, why don't you come with me? The speaker is very good and the singing is so full of life. It's like nothing you've ever heard. Trust me!"

I cleaned up after the supper rush at the restaurant and walked back to my room. Finally, after much deliberation, I decided to go.

We met at the front door of the hotel about fifteen minutes before the meeting was to start. It was bitterly cold and the wind-driven snow pelted us mercilessly as we walked down the block and around the corner to the hall. By the time we arrived our faces were stinging.

Stamping the snow from my boots and brushing it from my clothes, I looked around the hall. There were many familiar faces and it seemed everyone was talking with a neighbor or greeting those they hadn't seen for awhile. Quickly I made my way to the front row, with Mother's friend close behind.

A kind-looking gentleman made his way to the podium and raised his hands. When all was quiet, he thanked us for braving the cold and introduced himself as Reverend Erickson. I was so pleased he spoke English! By the time the second song began, I enthusiastically joined in the four-part harmony. The genuine joy that seemed to radiate from Pastor Erickson was far different from the ministers I had encountered in the past. I was all ears.

The message was wonderful! I had never heard anything like it, at least not that I could remember (or understand). He told us how God had sent His Son Jesus to die for our sins and how Jesus had risen from the dead and gone to heaven to be with His Father. Then he said that every one of us needed to be saved. I didn't know what that meant, but it seemed like a beautiful, warm and inviting concept—if it was true. Yet I found it confusing as well. It was that term "saved." I had heard very little about that word and certainly never in the way it was presented that evening.

Try as I might, I couldn't get to sleep that night. It felt like I was about to grasp something very important, but it was just beyond my reach. Finally, I drifted off. When I awoke the next morning, it was earlier than usual. Before going to work I quickly wrote a letter to Mom and Dad telling them about Reverend Erickson and his ability to preach the Bible in a unique way. I invited them to come and hear for themselves.

On Thursday night, I was pleasantly surprised to see them pull up in the bobsled. They had received my letter and decided to load the kids into the sleigh and come hear this man I had raved about, even though it was thirty-one degrees below zero.

They sat in the back, but once again I took my now customary seat in the front. The evangelist preached the same basic message he had given each previous night, but that Thursday evening his words seemed to penetrate my heart for the first time.

"Jesus paid the price for all of us on the cross," he said. "It was Jesus Christ, God's Son, who came to earth to die for all our sins. All we have to do is accept Him as our Savior and be saved."

There it was again. That word "saved"!

At the end of the service, Rev. Erickson gave an invitation to all those who wanted to accept Christ. Although I had felt no desire to go forward other nights, this night I desperately wanted to go. But instead, I gritted my teeth and remained glued to my seat. When the service ended, I sadly put on my coat and began to walk toward the exit. As I reached the door, I heard Mom call my name. I gave the family a quick wave, mumbled an excuse that I couldn't stay and talk and hurried out into the cold.

All at once, I burst into tears. By the time I reached the hotel, I was sobbing uncontrollably. I opened the door to the front of the building, buried my face in the fur collar of my coat and darted up the steps to my room.

Closing the door behind me, I slipped into my nightclothes, flung myself onto the bed and buried my face in the pillow. Sobs racked my entire body as I tried to cry myself to sleep. But try as I might, sleep would not come. I kept hearing over and over the words of the preacher: "Jesus paid it all on the cross. All you have to do is look up and ask Jesus to come into your heart."

Finally, after an immense struggle with God, I crawled out of bed just after midnight. With a remorseful, repentant and hopeful heart, I knelt down beside my bed.

"Oh God!" I began, "if there is such a thing as being saved, then do it!"

Never had the Creator heard a prayer more naive or childlike than the one I prayed that night—January 15, 1943. I was to find out later that we all must come to God as little children, regardless of our age or education.

As I once again climbed under the covers, a tremendous feeling of peace came over me. *What a miracle!* I thought. From sadness and loneliness to joy and love in the blink of an eye! From guilt and sin to peace and relief in an instant! It was an unbelievable sensation!

The next morning I awoke feeling refreshed and alive. There was a truly genuine smile on my face for the first time in a long while. That evening I went back to the hall. It was still a few minutes before starting time, when Reverend Erickson came to greet me.

"Hi! How are you this fine day, young lady?" he asked as he shook my hand.

"Very good," I replied somewhat shyly but with joy bursting inside me.

"I hope you won't mind if I ask you something," he said with a smile. I waited, not knowing what he was going to ask. "Did you accept Jesus Christ last night?"

I wasn't quite sure what he meant by that phrase, so I didn't say anything. There was a short uncomfortable pause. Sensing my unfamiliarity with the terminology he tried again. "Did you pray to God last night?"

My face lit up.

"Yes! Oh, yes! I did!" I blurted.

"That's wonderful!" he exclaimed glancing at his watch. "Listen, the meeting is about to start. Would it be possible for me to see you after the service tonight?"

Nodding, I told him that would be fine.

"Your name is . . . ?" he asked.

"Susan . . . Susan Dyck," I responded.

"Good! We'll see you after the service then, Susan."

That night Reverend Erickson again invited people to come to the front and publicly make a commitment to follow Christ. Then he added, "There may be some of you who didn't come forward other nights, but prayed to God at home later. If that was the case, why don't you come to the front as well so we can pray with you."

Instantly I shot out of my chair and almost ran to the platform. Others joined me and Reverend Erickson prayed with us all.

I wasn't the only one from my family to make a decision to follow Jesus that week. Thursday evening, Helen, Annie and Nick made the same commitment. Surprisingly, Dad thought that this repentance of sin was a good thing, at least for his kids. It wasn't like him to be so congenial about spiritual things. I was to find out later just how vehemently he could oppose Christianity.

A few months into my changed life, a missionary from South America came to Aberdeen. I went to hear him speak at the town hall. As usual, the building was jammed. He began by telling us how diligently he had worked over the past number of years, serving God. "In fact," he continued, "after all these years, what with working with so many different tribes, I probably know as many languages and dialects as there are people here this evening."

I gasped involuntarily. *There's no way that someone with as little education as me could ever be a missionary,* I thought to myself.

As the evening wore on, he spoke of the lepers and how they were shunned by society. His slides all too clearly revealed the suffering and pain in their eyes. I could not get them out of my mind. When he went on to tell us that these afflicted people had never heard of Christ I was horrified. I wanted desperately to go and tell them of my wonderful Savior. However, in my mind, missionaries were great people and I felt I had no hope of ever being able to meet such standards.

Sometime during the meeting I bowed my head and began to pray silently but fervently.

Oh, Lord! I began, *Please send some of these educated ones here tonight that they may serve You in the land of South America.*

"Forget those beside you," the missionary's voice implored. "It is not those next to you that need your prayers. It is you! You need to pray, 'Lord, here am I! Send me!' "

I was shocked! How could he know I was praying for others to go? The thought that God might actually want me to be a missionary was so far-fetched, I just shook my head and said quietly to myself, "I can't pray that. I'm not good enough or smart enough to go." So, once again I bowed my head, pleading with God to send someone.

Again I heard the missionary ask us not to pray for anyone but ourselves. Even though the room was full, it felt like this man was talking directly to me. I argued with God, but finally I could stand it no longer. For the third time I bowed my head. This time I poured my heart out to God.

"Lord, I do not know how you could use someone like me on the mission field. I'm such a young Christian, just a waitress with little education. But Jesus, if this is what You want, then here I am, send me!"

A few weeks later, Reverend Erickson arrived back in Aberdeen for another week of services. Through word of mouth he invited believers, especially those of us who had become Christians on his first visit, to come to a special meeting. So, on the Sunday afternoon before the evening meetings began, I went to the hall.

He told us about a blind man and how Jesus had restored his sight by placing clay moistened with His own spittle on his eyes. It was only after washing the clay off, he said, that the blind man's sight was restored.

"Do you know that the clay Jesus used in Palestine stuck to everything?" Rev. Erickson asked. "It was despised. When it was wet, it created a terribly sticky mess. However," he continued, "do you notice that in the hands of

Jesus that same clay becomes very useful and of much worth?"

Then, raising his voice slightly, he said, "People all over the world are spiritually blind and Jesus is looking for clay to open their eyes."

I felt as though I had been hit with a ton of bricks. Right then and there I knew I no longer had any choice in the matter. I bowed my head and wept before God and, as I did, a burning desire began building within me to do whatever God wanted me to do. I didn't know exactly what that might entail, but I didn't care. I knew He would choose only the best for me.

"Lord," I cried, "I volunteer to be that clay! I pray that the people I meet over the years will never give heed to this lump of clay. Rather, as You mold me, have them see only You, the Christ, and may they give all the praise to You."

My missionary journey was about to begin.

4

Praying Through

It was a beautiful autumn day in 1943 when I stepped off the train in Regina, the capital city of the province of Saskatchewan. To say that I was excited would have been a huge understatement. Being a small-town girl, I stared in wonder at the hustle and bustle of a big-city train station.

It took me a few minutes to retrieve my belongings—a couple of suitcases and two boxes, all bursting at the seams. One by one I carried them into the station.

Putting the last box down, I looked around. It hardly seemed possible that I was actually here, especially in light of the trouble my father had caused over the last few months. Although Dad was not opposed to my walking forward at the evangelistic meetings in Aberdeen, when I mentioned my intentions to attend Bible school, he became very angry, voicing his displeasure on numerous occasions. After one particularly heated argument, I decided to venture home only when necessary.

As the day of my departure drew near, Father and I remained distant. Although absolutely convinced that going to Bible school was the right thing to do, I still spent many an agonizing night in prayer, crying out to God that He would soften my father's heart. The Schroeders were a constant source of comfort and support and encouraged me not to turn my back on him. Fortunately, I was far too busy those final days in Aberdeen, packing and saying farewell to friends, to let Dad's lack of consent consume my thoughts.

Going through the checklist the school sent, I carefully packed everything they requested, including "a plain black dress with no trim and well below the knee" to be worn when representing the school on Christian Service assignments. White cuffs and collars and a small black bow tie were to be purchased on arrival at the school office, transforming our dresses into a kind of uniform. Since the school had no dormitories, it was necessary that we also bring light housekeeping supplies.

With the help of the Schroeders, I gathered my belongings and carried them down to the train station. Making sure it was all loaded in the baggage car, I said my last goodbyes and boarded the train. As it slowly pulled away from the quiet little town of Aberdeen I gazed

sadly out the window. Though excited about
what lay ahead, tears began to well up inside
when I thought how nice it would have been if
Dad had been there to see me off.

I looked back at the station, gave a final wave
to the Schroeders, then leaned back for the six-
hour ride to Regina. On any other day I probably
would have enjoyed the trip—the wide open
spaces, the wind gently caressing the tall prairie
grass, the hypnotic clickety-clack of the wheels
as they sped over the rails. But my heart was
heavy. I couldn't shake the pangs of loneliness,
nor the sense of rejection I felt from my father.

Then suddenly my thoughts were interrupted.
We were stopping at Clarkboro, the village
nearest our farm! I tried not to look out the
window, but curiosity got the better of me and
I decided to take one quick glance at the little
town I loved. On the platform, a few passengers were waiting to board and railway employees were loading the baggage car and water
tanks. As my eyes swept the length of the station's platform, a solitary figure caught my attention. It was Dad!

Jumping up from my seat, I quickly made my
way down the aisle, climbed off the train and
flew down the length of the platform to where
he was standing. He took one hesitant step toward me and then stopped. Slowing my pace, I
came to a halt in front of him.

"It's so good to see you, Dad!" I blurted, still
panting. I gazed apprehensively at him, trying

to gauge his feelings toward me. I wanted so much to reach out to him, but he remained aloof, standing stoically a few feet in front of me.

After a long and uncomfortable pause, he finally spoke.

"I thought you might need some meat." He thrust a box of Mennonite sausage in my direction.

"Oh, thank you, Dad. I sure could use it," I replied somewhat cautiously. Then, after a brief moment of hesitation, I forged ahead. "Thank you for coming to see me off, Dad. I'm so happy you came."

For one brief moment he appeared to soften. I actually thought he might give me his blessing. But then, just as suddenly, his face hardened. Pointing in the direction of the train, he said gruffly, "The train's getting ready to leave, Susan. You're going to miss it if you don't hurry."

Glancing over my shoulder, I dashed for the train and clambered aboard just as it began to pull away. I stood by the window watching. My father, tall and straight, remained on the platform a long time. Briefly I saw his hand move as though he was about to wave. Then, just as suddenly, he dropped it, turned around and slowly walked away.

I settled back into my seat and once again tried to make sense out of the feelings stirring inside me. I was thrilled that Dad had come to see me off. I knew he never would have come if

he didn't want to. But I couldn't help asking
God if my father would ever change.

The transportation from the school arrived. I
loaded my belongings in the car and climbed in
for the drive to school. The streets of Regina
were lined with more shops and businesses
then I had ever seen. On the corner of Osler
and Thirteenth stood a large, two-story brick
building—the Regina Christian and Missionary
Alliance Tabernacle, also the home of the Canadian Bible Institute, the only theological
training school for the Alliance in Canada. A
small insignificant sign—"Canadian Bible Institute"—was the only visible indication that an
educational center with eighty-seven students
and faculty members flourished within these
walls.

I could hear the sounds of many voices coming from the entrance at the bottom of the
stairs. I peeked around the corner. Many
young people like myself were lined up at various locations in a large open area. I learned
later that this room also served as a classroom,
chapel and dining hall!

When my turn finally came to speak to the
registrar, she smiled endearingly and introduced herself as Ruby Johnston. I warmed up
to her almost immediately. Then, it was on to
other lines to pay my tuition, receive my ac-
commodation assignment, choose my classes
and the type of Christian Service I would be in-

volved in—and meet the president of the school.

Not long after arriving at school I met a young woman who would become not only a close friend, but someone who would also have a significant and lasting impact on my spiritual life. Her name was Margaret Giguere.

This petite, beautiful, outspoken teenager was from Quebec. With lovely brown eyes, a vibrant and bubbly personality, it wasn't long before she became everyone's favorite. Her humor was contagious and she could preach like a house on fire. The fellows used to jokingly tell her that they couldn't marry her because she would probably outpreach them! Margaret and I became close friends.

Three weeks after meeting her, Margaret began talking to me about joining her for a night of prayer, Bible reading and fasting.

"A whole night of prayer!" I exclaimed in amazement.

"Sure! Why not?" she replied reassuringly. "A lot can be accomplished for God if people will take the time to talk to Him."

I wasn't yet totally convinced that a whole night of prayer was for me, so I asked Margaret where she spent these nights. She told me that the president of the school, Rev. George M. Blackett, allowed her to pray in the basement of the church. "In fact," she continued, "I often go and ask him what we should be praying for before I start. So, how about it, Susan? Would

you like to meet me at the church tomorrow
night?"

I thought it over for a moment, then nodded
my consent.

The next morning I awoke, still unsure of my
ability to stay awake the entire night let alone
find enough to pray about. As real as my
doubts were, it wasn't enough to hinder the
breaking of new ground in my relationship with
God. I sensed that something new was about
to happen in my life.

It was 9:30 when I arrived at the church. A
couple of people were quietly studying in various parts of the central room. As I waited for
Margaret to arrive, I wondered about the night
to come. I must have been deep in thought,
because the next thing I knew, I was all
alone—the church had suddenly become un-
comfortably quiet.

In less than five minutes I heard the door
open upstairs.

"Hi, Susan. Been waiting long?" Margaret
asked, depositing her coat at the bottom of the
stairs.

"No," I said in a hushed voice. "Boy, I'm glad
you got here. It's scary in this place all alone."
There was a short pause. "Some prayer warrior
I'm going to make, eh?" We both laughed.
"Well, how do we start?"

Without another word, Margaret went to the
chalkboard and began to write. As I watched,

these words appeared: "We are not here to dream or to drift. We are here because we have hard work to do, burdens to bear and loads to lift."

As the night wore on, I realized that I couldn't have found a more ardent, enthusiastic or serious-minded prayer warrior than Margaret Giguere. Watching her that first night, I learned what it meant to have a burden for people in need. Through her I learned how to cry out to the Lord, Master of heaven and earth, asking Him to save the lost and bring revival to the school. In my five years at CBI, it was those all-night prayer meetings that were my greatest joy.

When we began these prayer meetings there were a few things I needed to know. One of them I learned from Mr. Blackett: "Do not let people know when you have prayed, and do not speak about it freely in front of others." It was clear that he did not want our all-night prayer meeting to become an occasion for boasting.

So, after having spent a night in prayer, Margaret and I would go into the washroom, wash up, straighten our hair and clothes and be alert when teachers and other students arrived for the start of classes.

Another thing I discovered about these prayer nights was that, at times, they could be long and hard. When that happened, it was difficult to stay awake, especially if you were alone. The worst moment was around 3 a.m.

I remember one night in particular when God intervened and overcame my tiredness in a remarkable way. Margaret was unable to join me that evening and I was left to pray alone. Wanting to be close to where I could get a drink of water every once in awhile, I decided to pray in the kitchen.

As the night wore on I became extremely tired. Kneeling on the hard floor had taken its toll on my knees. It was also lonely. The only reason I didn't give up that night was because I knew there was no way I could get back into my apartment. So I pushed myself to continue.

However, just as I reached what I thought was my breaking point, something, or should I say Someone, suddenly lifted me up and gave me strength. I don't know how to describe it other than to say it appeared that there were angels all about me, sent from God, to lift my spirits. It was beautiful and comforting. It felt like I was in His hands and nothing could stop me from praying. So, with renewed strength, I prayed on.

My first year at CBI was truly a breath of fresh air compared to the first twenty years of my life. And, best of all, I discovered what it meant to pray until an answer comes. It was a discipline I would carry with me for the rest of my life.

However, it wasn't long before my prayer life was put to the test.

5

No Cloud in the Sky

D uring my first year at school, I sensed God leading me to be baptized by immersion. I had been baptized as a young girl after taking catechism classes, but, in my heart I didn't truly know Christ. I wanted to be baptized as a believer.

Rev. Murray Downey, one of the professors at the institute, agreed to come to Aberdeen and perform the baptism. The date was set and I anxiously anticipated the moment.

During the long train ride back home, I spent a great deal of time agonizing over what I would tell my parents. I knew my decision was the right one, but I didn't know how Dad would react or even how I should approach him on the subject.

I was met by my parents and the siblings still living at home. We spent several hours sharing what had been happening in our lives over the last year. Finally, at what I thought was an appropriate moment, I decided to inform Dad of my upcoming baptism.

He became very upset and tried to talk me out of it. But eventually, when he realized I was not going to change my mind, he told me in no uncertain terms that if I carried through with my decision, he would come and shoot both me and Mr. Downey! Whether that was an idle threat made in the heat of the argument, I didn't know. However, having seen the anger my father was capable of in the past, I knew his words could not be taken lightly. With a note of finality in his voice, he fired one last volley.

"Susan," he thundered, "if you get baptized, you can never come back to us. You can never come back to this house. You're no daughter of mine!"

Mom gasped and my resolve began to weaken. When I was a little girl, Dad had told us that children were to obey their parents, that it was in the Bible. So I really wasn't sure what to do next. In the end, I did what I had learned to do when faced with a painful situation—I left the house and made the short walk to Grandma's garden to be alone with God.

"Lord," I began quietly, "I don't know where to find Your will in this situation. Please lead me and tell me what to do. Should I obey my parents or get baptized?" I knew that if I

prayed and opened my Bible, God would
somehow lead me to the answer.

I opened my Bible and looked at the top of
the page. The caption read "Matthew Chapter
10." Immediately my eyes fell on the following
words:

> Anyone who loves his father or mother
> more than me is not worthy of me; any-
> one who loves his son or daughter more
> than me is not worthy of me; and anyone
> who does not take his cross and follow
> me is not worthy of me. Whoever finds
> his life will lose it, and whoever loses his
> life for my sake will find it. (Matthew
> 10:37-39)

I knew I had my answer. Thanking the Lord,
I walked back to the house, confident in what I
had to do. Mom and Dad were still in the
kitchen, his anger still evident.

"Father," I began, "I love you very much. I
love Mother very much too. But I love Jesus
more. And if that means I have to forsake my
parents to follow Jesus, then I'm going to follow Jesus."

Dad's eyes seemed to bore into my very soul.
Putting his hands together, he said, "Then I
don't know you any longer. You're none of
mine."

With no other recourse, I grabbed my suitcases and walked out into the yard. I had had

no time to think about my next move, but no sooner had I exited the house than a car drove into the yard. It was the Schroeders.

"Hi, Susan," Mr. Schroeder called as he stepped out of the car. "It's so good to see you again. My wife and I heard you were back, so we came to visit you and your folks."

"I'm sorry, you can't come in now," I said, shaking my head for emphasis. "It's not a good time. Please take me to Aberdeen, would you?"

Although obviously puzzled by my response, he lifted my suitcases into the trunk and I got into the backseat of the car. He had just turned the car around and began heading down the driveway when Dad came charging out of house.

"Susan!" he shouted. "Your mother has fainted and she might not live! Change your mind! Come back!"

I looked back at him. My mind was swirling. I was worried about Mother, but knowing that neither my father nor I were going to change our positions, I turned and faced the front of the car, an unbearable anguish tearing at my heart.

"Please, step on the gas," I pleaded with Mr. Schroeder.

"But why, Susan?" he asked doubtfully.

"Don't ask any questions!" I said. "Just step on the gas and go. I'll tell you later."

After a brief and bewildered look at his wife, Mr. Schroeder stepped on the gas and drove away, leaving my father standing alone, the dust from our tires swirling around him.

The Schroeders invited me for supper and then to the church service that evening. I thanked them, but graciously declined supper. Instead, I told them I'd meet them later at the church. I needed some time alone with God.

Walking a distance from their house, I found a bush and knelt beside it. I prayed for Mother, that she would be well. Then I cried out, "Lord, I have forsaken all to follow You. Now You must tell me what the next step is."

After much weeping and searching, I got up from behind the bush, ran to the house, made myself presentable and headed off to church. I tried to concentrate on what the minister said, but other thoughts rushed through my mind: *Where am I going to stay? Will Mom and Dad ever speak to me again? Is Mom OK?*

Back at the Schroeders, a car pulled into the driveway. It was the Krugers, a Christian family who was hiring me for the summer.

"Susan," said Mrs. Kruger, smiling warmly, "we just came from church and have stopped by to take you home with us tonight. You don't have to wait until your job begins. The Schroeders told us what happened."

"Oh, thank you," I replied, knowing that part of my prayer had just been answered.

When we got to their house, a few miles out of town, Mrs. Kruger said, "You must be tired, Susan. Come with me. I'll show you to your room." Then, putting her arm around me she whispered softly, "This will be your home until your parents meet you with blood-redeemed arms." I looked at her, tears filling my eyes. "Now, get some rest," she continued. "Feel free to sleep as long as you want." With that she gave me a little hug and made her way down the stairs.

I walked into the room and shut the door behind me. I was tired, but I knew I would not be able to sleep that night. So, I opened my Bible again and prepared for a full night of prayer. Casually I looked down at the page. "I will lie down and sleep in peace, for you alone, O LORD, make me dwell in safety" (Psalm 4:8).

It couldn't be that the Lord wants me to sleep, could it? I wondered. Quickly I scanned the earlier Psalm for confirmation. There, another verse popped out at me. "I lie down and sleep; I wake again, because the LORD sustains me" (Psalm 3:5). As I read that last verse a feeling of absolute peace swept over me.

"Lord! If You want me to sleep, I'll sleep. I know Your word says to follow You and I am doing that. So I leave everything in Your hands. I commit my mother to You. Please take care of her." I paused momentarily. "If You want me to sleep, I'll sleep," I repeated. "I'll do anything You want me to do."

With that I pulled back the covers, climbed into bed and within minutes fell into a deep sleep.

A day or two later I got a phone call from my father. Mom had recovered, but was still very disturbed that he had disowned me. During our brief conversation he announced somewhat abruptly, "Susan, you're mother wants us to come and see you."

A few days later they showed up at the door of the Kruger home. Even though things were tense, Dad was very cordial. We talked for some time, but Mom said very little, hoping things would work out between the two of us. After some discussion, Dad locked eyes with me.

"Susan, it's the devil that is causing you to do this. What you're doing—it's all wrong."

I sighed. I was tired and knew in my heart that we were getting nowhere. But I wanted this to end amicably, so we talked a little longer.

Then, suddenly, an idea began to formulate in my mind, something so wild and bizarre that if any of my friends had known about it in advance they would have immediately tried to talk me out of it. Deep inside, though, I knew that what I was about to say would end this discussion once and for all.

"Dad," I began confidently, "you say that I'm praying to the devil and that you are praying to God." He nodded. "Well, my baptism is set for this Sunday. If you feel that I am praying to the devil, why don't you and I both pray?"

Dad's brow furrowed. I continued.

"Why don't you pray for rain on Sunday, Father, and I'll pray it won't rain. If it rains on Sunday or even if there's but one cloud in the sky, I won't get baptized, OK?" At that moment I was so sure of what I was doing that I felt I could say anything and God would see me through!

Dad was shocked. But it was a challenge he couldn't refuse.

Later that day, when I informed the Schroeders and the Regiers of what I had done, they looked at me in stunned disbelief.

"I'm just following what God told me to do," I countered. "I know beyond a shadow of a doubt that He wants me to get baptized this Sunday. There will be no cloud in the sky. And even if my father does come to the baptism with the intention of shooting me and Mr. Downey, the bullets will go right past me. God has spoken to me and absolutely no harm is going to befall me."

I could tell they still didn't approve, but all that week they prayed that no cloud would appear on Sunday. I prayed but once. God was so close to me it felt as though He was standing at my side. I really couldn't understand the fuss everyone was making. After all, did God have any limits?

The next few days went by quickly. Friday or Saturday I received a call from the Bible school. They told me that one of the two girls who had signed up to go to Meadow Lake for the summer to work with Daily Vacation Bible School, was unable to make it. Would I be able to take her place? Even though I had planned to work for the Krugers the entire summer, they gave their consent.

On the day of my baptism, while I slept, my friends were up at 5 a.m. praying for a clear blue sky. I awoke around 8 feeling refreshed and looking forward to the day. I threw open the curtains and looked outside. There wasn't a cloud in sight!

It was an exciting day for me. God had answered my prayer as I knew He would. Later, when Pastor Downey baptized me in a dirty little lake a few miles from Aberdeen, I was overjoyed. I was making a commitment to God in front of the world, telling everyone that I was one of His children, ready to do whatever He wanted me to do.

And Dad? Well, he didn't interfere. In fact, I received no word from home and shortly thereafter I left for Meadow Lake, knowing nothing of my parents' reactions when they awakened that Sunday morning. All summer, every time I reflected on how they were doing, I had the sensation of a sword piercing my heart. Many days I walked up a hill and into the trees to spend time in prayer for Mom and Dad. And, faithfully I wrote every week or two, never receiving a reply.

As registration day for Bible school drew near, I continued to ask God for guidance:

Should I go home or go straight to Regina? To tell the truth, I was afraid to go home. Not having heard how Mom and Dad had reacted on the day of my baptism, I was a little leery of finding out.

Then one day, God spoke to me very clearly and gave me the assurance that I should go home. I wrote a letter telling my parents of my decision. Once again, I received no reply.

When the train pulled into the little village of Clarkboro I anxiously peered out the window. No familiar faces. I picked up my bags and got off. The platform was empty. As the sound of the chugging engine and the clickety-clack of the wheels moved off into the distance, I began to wonder if I had really heard from God.

It was less than a mile to the house. When I finally arrived at the bottom of the last hill, my courage wavered. I knew that once I reached the rise of the bluff in front of me, Mom and Dad would be able to see me. And, to put it bluntly, I was scared of the reception I would receive.

God! I can't do it! my mind cried out. I put my suitcases down and sat under a nearby bush. Slowly pulling my knees up, I buried my head in my hands and began to tremble.

"Lord, I have no courage!" I finally cried. "What if my father is just as angry as ever? I know maybe this is too much to ask, but I need one more sign of comfort, anything that will tell me this is what You want me to do. Whatever You say, I'll do."

With that desperate cry out of the way, I retrieved my Bible from the top of one of my suitcases and opened it. I read the story of the prodigal son, how, after he returned, there was great rejoicing. I raised my eyes toward the heavens. "Lord, I'll go! I believe You. There will be rejoicing!" I knew that in my case the roles of father and child were reversed, but the principle remained the same—the reuniting of a family.

Quickly I gathered my belongings and ran up the hill. At the crest, I paused to catch my breath. I gazed toward our farm nestled in the valley below. There were my parents standing by the driveway looking in my direction.

I began running down the hill as fast as I could. Mom started to run to meet me. As I neared them, I came to a halt, nearly out of breath. I could see that Mother was dying to hug me, as I was her. But she waited for Father to make the first move.

He took a step forward, put out his great big hand and said softly, "Welcome home, Susan." I ran toward him and grasped his hand with both of mine. At the same time, Mom threw her arms around me, clinging to me tightly.

"Oh, Susan!" she cried, the words tumbling from her lips, "there was no rain anywhere! Not a cloud in the sky! You were right and we were wrong. We know that you are following the Lord."

Dad said nothing, but she didn't care. The dam had burst. With her arm around me, she led me back to the house. Dad picked up my suitcases and followed close behind. "No cloud in the sky. You were right and we were wrong!" she repeated over and over again.

That night I pulled out one of the flannelgraphs I had used in teaching Vacation Bible School. Mother listened eagerly as I related story after story. I told her of the love of Jesus, how He had died for us and rose again; how we could ask Him to forgive our sins, choose to follow Him and then become His child. Finally, after many stories, my mother exclaimed, "I can understand it! You can be saved and know it! Oh, that's wonderful, Susan!"

Right there in the living room, we knelt together and she asked God to save her through the cleansing blood of His Son Jesus Christ.

I wish I could tell you that my father received Christ that day as well, but it was not to be. The months wore on and he continued drinking.

6

Something Specific

I awakened to the sounds of running feet as the girls scurried back and forth between their rooms and the washroom. It had been almost four years since the day of my baptism. And now, here I was about to graduate.

Three years earlier, during the fall of '45, the school had moved downtown to a new location at the old Clayton Hotel on 1720 Broad Street. For years Mr. Blackett had been praying for and dreaming of a building that would house the increasing number of students attending the institute. The need to relocate became even more acute as the war drew to a close and servicemen indicated their intention to attend CBI.

The Clayton Hotel was a three-story building located one block south of the train station, in the heart of downtown Regina. When the basement was renovated the following year, it provided a much needed fourth floor. All in all, our new home was a welcome change from the cramped quarters of the previous years.

The story of how God provided the hotel began near the end of my second year at school. One day, Margaret went to Mr. Blackett to ask if there was anything in particular that she and I could pray for. *

"Well, what did he say?" I asked excitedly as we settled into our usual spot in the basement.

"We're praying for only one thing tonight," she responded in all seriousness. "Mr. Blackett told me that he can't run this school any longer unless we get a building where we can all be together. So he wants us to pray that God will provide a place before the next term, one large enough to house our classes, dorm rooms and offices."

Talk about a prayer meeting for things thought impossible! Here it was only a few short weeks before the end of our present school year, with no money designated for a new building, and Mr. Blackett wanted it by the fall!

As we began to pray we searched our lives to ensure that we were coming to the perfect God with clean hearts.

"Susan," Margaret said, "I think tonight we should pray till it is perfectly clear to us that God is going to make a building available."

I nodded in agreement. That began a night of prayer the likes of which I had never witnessed before. Repeatedly Margaret thrust her hands into the air, pleading with God about our desperate need.

We took turns reading His Word, praying and singing. Finally, around 3 a.m., I said, "I'm sure, Margaret! God has given me the assurance that He will provide us with a building."

"Are you positive?" she asked excitedly.

"Yes, I'm positive," I replied, my voice rising with excitement. "As we were praying just now, a wonderful peace came over me. I can't explain it, but I know the building will be available by fall."

Margaret was happy for me, but as yet didn't have that same assurance. So she asked if I would lay hands on her and pray for her. I did, and then we continued to commune with God. An hour or two later, she finally looked up.

"God just doesn't give me assurance, Susan," she said. "Maybe we should ask Him for a sign. I know it's not good to ask for signs, but Gideon did it in the Bible, so why can't we do it too?"

"OK," I replied somewhat hesitantly. "What should we ask for?"

"Well," Margaret said, "let's make it something specific." There was a short pause, as we both considered the options.

"I know!" she finally shouted. "Let's ask God for a large amount of money to arrive at the school in three days, designated for the building fund. That'll give the mail plenty of time to arrive from almost anywhere in Canada and the U.S.

And listen, Susan, let's not tell anyone else what we've been praying for or what sign we've asked God for. Otherwise, when God answers this prayer, we might become conceited. OK?"

I nodded.

Around 6 in the morning, Margaret finally received the assurance that God would answer.

Two days passed. On the morning of the third day we assembled in the chapel. The stately Mr. Blackett appeared at the door and walked to the front.

"I have an announcement to make," he said, beaming with pleasure. Holding up an envelope for all to see, he continued. "A large sum of money came in this morning by mail from the U.S. The donor has designated it for our new building!"

Nudging Margaret, I leaned over and whispered in her ear, "Isn't God wonderful! I guess it's time for an all-night praise meeting tonight. Right?"

"Sh-h-h," she said putting her finger to her lips, smiling in agreement all the same. "Remember, let's not tell anyone. We don't want to get conceited."

Things moved rapidly after that. Miraculously, the Clayton Hotel came up for sale. On May 8, 1945, the day everyone celebrated the end of World War II, three men walked into the empty beer parlor of the hotel and stood in the middle of that huge room: Rev. George M.

Blackett, president of the (Western) Canadian Bible Institute, Rev. Gordon A. Skitch, district superintendent and chairman of the board, and Rev. W.H. Brooks, professor of Alliance Truth and Testimony. With the whistles of peace sounding throughout the city, they bowed their heads and humbly committed the building to God's work.

By August 15 the school had raised the necessary down payment to purchase the property. And by September 28, at 9 a.m. when the new school term began, the building had been "transformed from wine to worship, from beer to the Bible and from blasphemy to blessing" (1946 *Challenger* yearbook).

It was graduation week. My father arrived and the Downeys graciously allowed him to stay with them. I had stopped praying for his salvation by then because of an eventful night of prayer a couple of months earlier.

I decided to have an all-night prayer meeting by myself. So, about 10 o'clock that night, I made my way down to one of the soundproof music rooms in the basement. After many hours on my knees, I finally stood up, leaned face first against the wall and cried out to God.

"Lord," I began, "my father hasn't known anything but misery, pain and a distrustful spirit all his life. I can't take his pain any longer. I don't know if my father can be saved." I wept. "He seems to be getting worse and worse. Most of the others in my family have become Christians, but not Dad. I keep wondering if it's too late for him. Some of my brothers and sisters feel he has gone too far, but I don't believe it, Lord. Nothing is impossible for You!"

I took a deep breath, contemplating my next words. Then I continued.

"Lord, we have prayed so long now. If You can't save my Dad, I'll . . . I'll go to hell with him. I don't want to go to heaven without him." By this time my tears were running down the cement wall.

No sooner had my mouth uttered those words than my heart was filled with a glorious peace. As though He was standing right next to me, the Lord said, "Before you leave for the mission field, your dad will be saved."

"Oh, thank you, God!" I shouted. "I will never ask You again. Never! From now on I will only praise You for the answer already given."

Graduation came and went. After it was over, my Aunt Agatha came to me.

"Susan, isn't it time you started thinking about getting married?" she asked.

"No, Aunt Agatha," I replied. "I have no time for that."

At the time I didn't realize the full weight of those words. That would come later.

7

The Answer

As my three years of home service (at Lethbridge, Entwhistle and Magnolia, Alberta) drew to a close, my hopes and dreams of going overseas were suddenly shattered. A letter from the Alliance headquarters informed me that because of a lack of funds they would be unable to send me. Although it was no consolation, I discovered that I wasn't the only one to experience this setback. It seemed there were dozens of single women like myself who were caught in the same financial shortfall.

After the initial disappointment, my resolve to go only intensified. So I wrote the district office, asking if I could raise my own support. Two weeks later they informed me that my plan was acceptable providing I would raise the money among churches and friends who were not affiliated with our denomination.

For the following two years I traveled throughout North America, speaking to various congregations about the Sulu Islands in the Philippines, the field to which I felt God was calling me. It had always been my hope that I would someday be able to join Mr. DeJesus, the missionary I had prayed for in Bible school.

During a winter in Toronto I received news that my new placement was Japan, Land of the Rising Sun. Apparently, because of political unrest in the Philippines, single missionaries were no longer being sent there. This came as a huge disappointment after so many years of praying for the country and its people.

I was scheduled to speak at the Avenue Road Alliance Church in Toronto (now Bayview Glen Church) when the news reached me. Knowing absolutely nothing about my new destination, I wondered what I would share. Fortunately someone gave me a pamphlet called "Scan of Hiroshima," which spoke of the unbelievable suffering the people of that region had endured since the nuclear blast that leveled their city.

As I read the heart-wrenching description of their plight, I instantly fell in love with the Japanese people. By the time I spoke a few nights later, I knew God had given me a burden for Japan. I don't remember exactly what I said or how long I spoke. However, when I sat down, people were weeping. Not fully understanding the reason for this emotional response, I turned to the lady next to me. "Why is everyone crying? Is there a revival going on?"

"You innocent child," the lady replied lovingly, "it's because of you and your words that people are crying. You touched a great many hearts here tonight."

I was stunned. Here I was, talking to a group of people about a country I knew nothing about and they had been totally overcome by the words God had given me. Many people stayed until midnight that night, consumed with the burden of helping the Japanese people. They also gave generously to my support, above and beyond their regular giving to Alliance missions.

Two weeks before my departure I went home one last time. When I stepped off the train in Clarkboro that wintry afternoon, Dad was there with the horses and sleigh, waiting for me. Even though it was well into March, a foot of snow still covered the ground.

Seeing him standing there on the station platform brought back a flood of memories. I realized that many things had happened since the day God gave me the assurance Dad would accept Jesus as his Savior before I left for the mission field. In fact, there were many times it seemed hopeless.

Oh, it was true that Dad's anger toward Christianity had subsided, but his body was beginning to pay the price for his indulgences. In fact, he no longer had control over his vices. He was trying to change, but he refused any help, be it from people or God.

Although it was a happy reunion, unfortunately it was not to last. Even though Dad had known of my plans to go overseas, he had refused to believe that I would actually do it. That's why, after loading my suitcase into the back of the sleigh, helping me climb in and wrapping some warm blankets around us both, he brought up the subject. When he discovered that my intentions had not changed, and that I was still determined to head for Japan, he folded his arms in disgust.

"Over my dead body!" he snarled through his teeth. Needless to say, the rest of the trip was chilly in more ways than one. The only sounds were those made by the horses hooves and the runners as they glided over the freshly packed snow.

The rest of the family was waiting for us when we pulled into the driveway. At first I was received warmly, but when Dad informed them that I was indeed on my way to Japan, a coolness settled over the room. It puzzled me, since many of my family had by now found faith in Christ.

"Listen everyone," I finally pleaded, looking at each of them, "could we go into the living room and talk? I've got something very important to say."

After a brief pause that seemed like an eternity, they filed quietly into the living room and sat down. All eyes turned to me. I took a deep breath, opened my Bible and began to read. I don't remember exactly what I read. I only know that it spoke of serving God and about the burden that we as Christians must have for others.

When I finished, I looked up.

"It means so much to me to see you again. I know it's hard for you to understand why I'm going away and it's difficult for you to let me go. But I know I am doing what God wants me to do." I paused. A long, uncomfortable silence followed. "I'm not going to see you again for six years," I continued. "It would mean so much if you would pray with me this one last time."

You could have cut the air with a knife. I felt like a bird trapped in a cage, battling a tremendous urge to be free. Over the next few minutes I poured my heart out to God, begging Him to help my family understand that it was He who was calling me and that I had no desire but to obey Him. I ended by praying for both their safety and mine.

As I finished I heard someone sobbing. My eyes widened with surprise. There was Dad, his hands buried in his face, crying uncontrollably. It was as if years of bitterness, anger and despair were finally being released. I don't think I ever heard a more cleansing sound.

Then suddenly, between sobs, he burst out in prayer.

"Oh, Father," he began. "You gave us this beautiful daughter. And we have done nothing but persecute her all these years. You didn't only die for her. You died for us all!"

I couldn't believe what I was hearing! For years I had prayed for this. And now, here it was! Oh, the joy in my heart that day! It was as if a heavy burden was lifted from my shoulders. Tears came to my eyes and I did nothing to hold them back.

I wish I could remember everything else Dad prayed that day, but having heard his first words of repentance, nothing else seemed important. He ended his prayer with these words, "Now, Father, I give Susan back to You and I give her to the people of Japan. Amen!"

The next two days were wonderful. With Dad's acceptance of me, the family seemed to breathe a corporate sigh of relief. There was a happiness and a release which had never existed. When the time came for me to leave, I kissed Dad goodbye. What a good feeling it was to finally have him accept my kiss and return the love.

Although Dad continued to solidify his newfound faith in Christ, he still continued to drink. Then in 1962, while he and Mom were traveling back from Saskatoon, they were in a car accident. Whether or not his drinking caused the accident, we do not know, but Dad believed it had. For the first time he had hurt someone as a result of his drinking, or so he thought, and it affected him deeply. The fact that it was Mother made it all the more troublesome.

That night, God's Spirit began to deal with him. After spending several hours in agonizing and repentant prayer, he finally found peace with God and forgiveness for his drinking. He died about six months later, ten years after I left for Japan.

We were thrilled that he was now delivered from his temptations forever, entering instead into a glorious life in heaven, forever with his Lord.

8

The Letter

"Susan, it's Sunday. Easter morning. Do you feel any better?" It was a woman's voice. "If you do," she continued, "I can get you something for breakfast and then we can go to the sunrise service."

The last thing I wanted was food. Shaking my head I mumbled, "No . . . not hungry. . . . I don't want to go to church."

I had arrived in Oakland, California the night before, already sick with a fever and sore throat. The Home of Peace was a stopping off place for missionaries who were either returning from or leaving for the mission field from San Francisco harbor.

Assuring everyone that I did not need someone to watch over me, the staff left for the service. Throughout the day I tossed and turned as the fever burned within. And, as I drifted in and out of sleep, a fear began to grip me, a fear that I might have polio. Polio was rampant in those days and a cure or prevention had not yet been discovered. Besides, wanting so badly to go to the mission field, I knew I would be unable to fulfill my dream if I had that dreaded ailment.

Sometime around 3 in the afternoon, the darkness of my room was disturbed once more as the door opened.

"Susan," one of the staff members called gently. I opened my eyes. Pointing to a man beside her, she continued. "This gentleman is here to help you with your papers and get your belongings ready for the trip. He has something important to tell you."

My eyes shifted in his direction.

"If you have any hope of getting on your ship by Tuesday afternoon," he said, "we have got to begin work on your papers today. If we don't start by 4 o'clock, Susan, I doubt if we can complete everything in time."

There were numerous papers to be signed, lists to be checked, last minute items to be purchased, etc., etc. And then, when that was done, everything had to be loaded on the ship by 3 p.m. It would have been an almost impossible task to complete even for a healthy person.

"We'll make it," I whispered, my voice rasping like sandpaper. "God wants me to go to Japan and He'll get me there."

They looked at me sympathetically, then, shaking their heads, they quietly left the room.

Four o'clock came and went and still there was no improvement. If anything, I was worse. The people from the home checked on me once more, but left just as quickly.

Another hour passed with no change. In desperation I began to question God. "Why? Why now, Lord? Don't You realize I need to be on that boat in less than two days?" I continued for a few moments until, out of the blue, a thought came to me: the fourfold gospel! Our Alliance motto!

As the words "Jesus Christ: Savior, Sanctifier, Healer and Coming King" unfolded before me, I thanked God for my salvation, for filling me with His Holy Spirit and for the joy and challenge of occupying till He comes again. Then I thought about the words, "Christ our Healer." My heart stopped! I realized I had never truly been sick before, at least not under such pressing circumstances. And, on top of that, I had never asked God to heal me physically.

If Christ is my Savior, Sanctifier and Coming King, I thought, *He is also my physical Healer.* "Lord!" I cried out, "I now take You as my Healer." Instantly the fever broke and I fell into a deep and restful sleep.

I awoke hours later surrounded by complete darkness. Hopping out of bed, I stretched and turned the light on. I felt refreshed and ready to go. Glancing at the clock on my night table, I couldn't believe it. Just a few short hours ago I had been miserable. Now, here it was 10 o'clock and I felt wonderful—and insatiably hungry!

Peeling off my pajamas, which were sopping wet from the effects of the fever, I dressed and ran downstairs.

"I'm healed! I'm healed! I can make the boat on Tuesday after all!" I shouted all the way to the bottom.

After the initial excitement died down, the gentleman I had spoken to earlier asked, "Susan, are you willing to work late into the night?"

"Oh, yes!" I exclaimed enthusiastically. "I'll work all night if that's what it takes." And so began the tedious job of completing the paperwork.

Later, after a little sleep and a quick breakfast, I continued my preparation by going over the medicine list. I thought of what we had been told, how everyone going overseas got worms and parasites if they didn't take certain prescribed medicines. As I read the long list of medical supplies, I suddenly heard the Lord say to me, "Susan, can you trust Me alone?"

Instantly, without another thought, I tore up the list and happily cried out, "Lord! I'll trust You only! I'll have no other doctor but You!" Then God gave me a verse: "They will pick up snakes . . . and . . . it will not hurt them . . . ; they will place their hands on sick people, and they will get well" (Mark 16:18).

Finally, on Tuesday, April 7, 1953, just after 3 p.m., we arrived at the pier where the *Maticat* was berthed. I was the last passenger to register. However, as my belongings were being stored in the hold, I suddenly realized I had forgotten to purchase a typewriter. The captain informed me that our departure time was 8 p.m. sharp. I looked down at my watch. It was only 4. Promising that I would be back before the appointed time, the captain gave me permission to go ashore. I scurried off the ship, down the pier and into a commercial area nearby. Eventually, I found a stationary store and bought a portable typewriter along with a few other incidentals.

When I finally reached the entrance to the pier, the gates were padlocked! No one was around and there appeared to be no way to get in. *What am I going to do, Lord?* I thought. *I've just got to make it to the ship.*

I checked the gate. There wasn't enough room to crawl under, and the top was protected with barbed wire, not that I would have been able to climb up there anyway.

"Lord, show me what to do," I prayed desperately. A couple hundred yards or so down the fence, I saw what appeared to be a small opening. Quickly I pushed my packages through the hole and crawled in after them. I brushed myself off and began running down the darkened pier. I couldn't see my watch and had no idea how much time I had wasted.

Finally, having resigned myself to the fact that I was going to miss the departure time, I saw a few dim lights ahead. It was the *Maticat!* Just as the sailors were lifting the gang plank, I shouted, "Wait for me! I need to get on that boat!"

There was a bit of muttering and grumbling as they lowered the gangplank and I scurried on. I made my way to the cabin that I was to share with a Japanese lady. Exhausted, I undressed and crawled into my bunk.

During the trip I was able to share my faith with everyone on board, including the captain and his crew. Some of the crew and a few women passengers were skeptical. But God—and the weather—were about to change that!

We were only two days outside of Yokohama harbor when a ferocious storm began to lash at us with ever-increasing intensity. The tiny ship shuddered against incredible pressure as the giant waves came crashing down upon it.

The first day the cook continued to prepare meals, but none of the passengers except me were able to enjoy them. That night though, the storm increased in intensity. By the next morning there was general concern for our safety. I could see it in the eyes of the sailors as they talked below deck. The ship rocked and shook violently as the winds took on what seemed like hurricane proportions. As wave after wave struck the ship's nose, plunging it into the sea, the crew watched and waited to see if she would recover. She would shudder, then slowly raise herself up and prepare for the next onslaught. Cargo lashed to the decks was lost. Even the cabin furniture tore loose from its bindings as the ship rocked violently to and fro.

When morning came, the *Maticat* was still afloat and, for a third day, she braved the fury of the storm. More cargo was lost. Water continued to fill the cabins. I passed one of the sailors in the corridor as I made my way to the cabin.

"Did you pray last night?" he asked respectfully.

"I always pray," I replied calmly. "Did you?"

"We all did," he responded, "and it looks like it helped. We thought we were going down last night."

The morning of the fourth day saw the skies relatively clear, the wind and waves less fierce. So we set about cleaning up and repairing what we could to make the ship a little more seaworthy and somewhat presentable when we docked. The men of the *Maticat* also treated me with a great deal more respect for the remainder of the journey.

We finally managed to limp into Yokohama, a battered but grateful group. A trip that was to have lasted two weeks took almost three. It felt good to have my feet firmly planted on ground once again.

There was an airmail letter from my father awaiting me. In it he stated how he had seen a vision of a storm and had prayed that God would see me safely through it. He closed by saying, "I pray that God will make you a light to all Japan."

It was April 24, 1953.

9

"Me, Same Same"

Paul and Helen McGarvey were there to meet me. They had arrived only six weeks earlier to reopen the Alliance Mission which had been closed during World War II. Miss Mabel Francis and her sister Mrs. Anne Dievendorf, who had been interned until the Japanese surrender in 1945, had also returned. (See *One Shall Chase a Thousand*, Christian Publications.) It was largely because of the insistence of these two ladies that I arrived in Japan when I did. Swamped with caring for the traumatized population of Hiroshima, they requested that another woman be commissioned to help them. In response to their plea, Paul McGarvey sent a telegram to the Alliance headquarters in New York. It read simply, "Send Dyck!" So, here I was.

It wasn't long before I discovered that Japan is a country made up of four major islands and nearly a thousand smaller ones. The Sea of Japan separates it from Korea and the former Soviet Union. The major islands extend for 1,300 miles (2,100 kilometers), the largest and most heavily populated being the Island of Honshu where I would spend most of my thirty-two years as a missionary. Another island, Hokkaido, lay to the north of Honshu, with Kyushu and Shikoku to the south.

When I arrived in Kobe, a city of 1 million, for language study, it was, like many places in Japan, still reeling under the devastating aftermath of the war. It had been only eight years since Japan's surrender and a year since the official end of the Allied occupation. Many Japanese were still struggling to put their lives back together and some were living in extreme poverty.

I must admit I really did not want to go to Japan. I didn't think I was educated enough to learn such a difficult language nor work with such a sophisticated people. Fortunately though, after being commissioned, God gave me a verse of encouragement that allayed my fears: "And these signs will accompany those who believe: In my name they will drive out demons; *they will speak in new tongues . . .*" (Mark 16:17, emphasis added). From the moment I read that verse I claimed it as my own and threw myself wholeheartedly into learning

Japanese, knowing that God would give me this new tongue.

However, a month or so into my schooling I was told that my voice did not have the musical qualities necessary to speak Japanese acceptably. But I persisted, and in the end my hard work paid off and I completed the course on schedule.

During those months in Kobe, I didn't have a great deal of time to do much more than study. However, while visiting some friends in a neighboring town, a very special event took place. I was asked to give my testimony at an evangelistic service. With the help of an interpreter, I told the story of how I was saved and how most of my family had become Christians. I explained how we had prayed for my father for eleven years and how, on the day I left, he had given me back to the Lord and promised that he would serve God.

When I finished speaking, a Japanese lady stepped forward.

"My mother was a Christian," she said, "and although she prayed for me for many years, I have never yielded to Christ. Tonight, when I heard you tell about praying for your father for so long, I was reminded of my mother's prayer. I want to give my life to the Christ." I wrote home: "Dad, you were the cause of my first convert in Japan!"

Sometime later, circumstances led me to cross paths with the individual who had predicted that I might never learn the language. When she heard me talk, she exclaimed, "Oh, Susan! I just love to hear you speak Japanese! It's so beautiful!" Whether true or not, her words were the praise I needed at that moment. It was also a sign to me of God's continued faithfulness and direction in my life.

My first assignment was in the city of Fukuyama, sixty miles east of Hiroshima. Out of all the exciting things that happened to me in Fukuyama, one incident stands out.

When Anne Dievendorf left for the U.S. I took over her English class comprised of high school and university students and some career gentlemen. One of them was Mr. Sato, an engineer with an international technological company.

As Christmas drew near, I determined to do something special for my newfound friends. So, one day at the beginning of the class I invited them and their wives to a North American-style Christmas dinner. Everyone except Mr. Sato seemed responsive to the idea.

Later, when the class concluded, he stayed behind.

"Miss Dyck," he began cordially, "I want you to know that I would be honored to come to your house for dinner. But I'm afraid it just won't be possible."

"Why not?" I asked, puzzled at his obvious discomfort.

"My wife is a very strong Buddhist, Miss Dyck," he said hesitantly. "She absolutely hates anything whatsoever to do with Christianity. I'm afraid it will be impossible for me to bring her." I could tell he was genuinely disappointed and a little ashamed of his wife's feelings toward Christians.

"Well, you tell your wife that I would very much like to meet her," I countered. "Would you please try?"

The next several days saw me scurrying about planning for a Christmas dinner with all the "fixins." I wanted it to be as close to a traditional North American meal as possible so they could experience not only our food but our customs as well. Unable to locate any turkeys, I roasted four chickens. To that I added mouth-watering stuffing, creamy mashed potatoes, several kinds of vegetables, a big pot of steaming gravy and apple pies—the kind Mother used to make.

To my complete surprise, Mr. Sato appeared at the door with his wife! I greeted her warmly, but I couldn't help noticing her overwhelming sadness. I had grown accustomed to seeing such despair in the faces of the Japanese, but I still found it disconcerting. It wasn't hard to figure out why they felt the way they did. Their country was in ruins and many had lost loved ones in the war. On top of that, they were ashamed of defeat. It was as if the whole country was still in mourning and had forgotten how to smile.

When the last guest arrived, I showed them to their seats around the tables and asked them to speak English only if possible. Then I explained western table manners. If they wanted something from the table they were to ask those nearest the food to pass it. They agreed but looked somewhat askance at the spread before them.

I knew that, especially for elaborate meals, Japanese custom dictated that each individual be provided with his or her own set of serving dishes and a set of chopsticks. The dishes were then placed in a semicircle around each setting. Once the meal began, it was not considered proper etiquette to dip your chopsticks into a bowl of food you had no intention of finishing.

However, there was another reason for their reticence. If there is one thing that bothers Japanese people, it is the sight of bones at a meal. It is considered poor etiquette in their culture. But it had been a long time since some of them had witnessed a feast like the one in front of them, so they determined to make the best of it and overlook a few unsightly bones.

As we began to eat, I once again explained in English how to pass things around, but for some reason my instructions were largely ignored. The charade that followed was amusing. Whenever someone wanted something, they just reached over. One fellow in particular almost put a knee on the table stretching for a platter! I kept trying to explain how to pass the food, but eventually gave up, at first snickering as discreetly as possible at the antics, then finally bursting out laughing.

We had a marvelous time! Later, when Mr. and Mrs. Sato returned home, Masako told her husband, "I want to learn to laugh and have sparkling eyes like Miss Dyck."

"That's foolishness, Masako," her husband replied. "The only reason Miss Dyck has sparkling eyes and is able to laugh like that is because she loves Christ. You hate Christ! You don't like Christianity! You have told me that yourself many times. And, if you're not a Christian, you can't laugh like that."

"Well, if that is what it takes to get sparkling eyes and laugh like Miss Dyck, I want to become a Christian too," she replied with a sense of finality in her voice.

A few days later I answered a knock at my door. There was Mrs. Sato. After inviting her in and exchanging pleasantries, she informed me that she wanted to become a Christian like me.

"Oh, Mrs. Sato!" I exclaimed, "that's terrific!"

My hands started to shake as I opened my Japanese Bible. I had underlined the key verses for helping someone receive Christ as their Savior. Slowly, one by one, I encouraged her to read them. Then I explained what it meant to have Jesus take control of her life. One of the last verses we read was, "Whosoever shall call upon the name of the Lord shall be saved" (Romans 10:13, KJV). As we finished reading, she indicated that it was her wish to accept Jesus as her Savior.

It hardly seemed possible that this was the same woman who, just a few short weeks ago, had vehemently announced her hatred for Christianity. Now here she was with head bowed, sitting in my living room, giving her heart to Jesus. It was a miracle! Nothing short of a miracle! Immediately she pointed to my Bible and said in broken English, "Me, same same." All I had was a New Testament, so I gave it to her.

For two weeks I didn't see her again. Just as I was deciding to investigate how she was doing, she appeared at my door again. Explaining that she had finished reading the New Testament from cover to cover, she asked, "What next?"

I asked if she had understood everything she read. She said, "No, not all of it."

"OK," I responded. "Now what I want you to do is read the first four books again, the Gospels." She nodded her agreement. "I want you to read them one at a time and mark down anything you don't understand. Then come and see me again and I will try to explain whatever it is you don't understand."

At one of our meetings during the following month, she said excitedly, "Miss Dyck, I have many friends in my husband's company. I want you to come with me to the apartment compounds where they live and tell them

about Jesus." Those compounds were comprised of large, high-rise, company-built
apartment buildings filled with thousands of
people.

"OK," I said, "that sounds like a good idea.
But I'm going to need a bicycle in order to get
around to all of them."

"No problem," she said in English. "I help
buy." Then pointing at herself, she continued,
"Me, same same!" She helped me search for a
suitable bike, then we both bought one exactly
the same.

During the next year we spent many a day
traveling from compound to compound con-
tacting the wives of the company employees
while their husbands were at work. Usually it
happened like this. Upon arriving at a particular complex, Masako would contact her closest
friend in the building, asking if we could use
her apartment for an informal meeting to listen
to a missionary friend with a lovely story to tell.
Having received permission, she would then
begin running up and down the stairs and hall-
ways. "Come quickly!" she would say. "A lady
from Canada has come and has a message you
have never heard."

In almost every case we spoke to a full house.
Having memorized key verses from Genesis to
Revelation, I very simply explained how God
had made us in His image, how we had fallen
into sin, how God loved people so much that
He sent His Son to die for us and how through

Christ's resurrection He had paid the price for us all. When I got stuck with the language, Masako came to my aid.

Hardly a day went by that we didn't lead someone to Christ. Before long, forty ladies had made that decision. And, as the months went by, a few husbands became Christians too.

I left Fukuyama in the fall of 1955. Mr. Sato received a promotion and transferred to Tokyo. Throughout the years though, no matter where I went, Masako continued to support my work. And when she had a problem or just wanted to talk, she would often call me long distance.

I wish I could say that Mr. Sato became a devout believer. All I can say is that he professed to be a Christian. Whether or not he really followed Christ faithfully, I never knew.

10

The Worst Man in Town

Matsue was no more than 100 miles from Fukuyama as the crow flies. However, the trip took nearly eight hours as the train slowly wound it's way north to the Sea of Japan and through the Chugoku Mountains with their many tunnels, bridges and long winding climbs.

The house that fellow missionary Hilda Snider and I rented was typically Japanese, with a spacious veranda running along two sides and sliding doors on the exterior walls giving easy access to the adjacent rooms. Although most of the house was quite pleasant, the kitchen was an entirely different matter. Coming from rural Saskatchewan where the kitchen was the most important, spacious and brightly decorated room in the house, I found it extremely difficult to get used to the cold, dingy cubicle. Soot covered the concrete floor. There were no cupboards, little or no furniture and no room for the refrigerator which we moved into the already overcrowded living room.

Open to the attic, the kitchen was also a haven for rats. I could hear them scurrying overhead while I cooked, and at night I would listen as they made their way down the walls to raid the potato bin and macaroni supply. It got so bad that in order to keep them quiet I'd climb up into the rafters and drop off "something nice" for them to eat. It was a whole year before we were able to renovate the room and make it more to our liking—closed-in ceiling, new sink and taps, a linoleum floor and fresh paint on the walls. After that, the rats stayed upstairs in the attic and the kitchen became somewhat cozy—as long as one could live with the pitter-patter of little feet!

Hilda and I threw ourselves into our ministry in Matsue and the outlying areas—comforting those with tuberculosis, visiting in the prison, planting churches and holding tent meetings. Although missionary work was rewarding, there were times we had to endure many hardships that led to physical illness, emotional stress or just plain frustration.

One of those frustrations, believe it or not, was the laundry. At times the humidity was so high that clothes wouldn't dry on the line and either molded or rusted on the hangers. Even freshly baked bread would turn moldy by the end of the day.

The constant threat of persecution was also mentally draining, not only for the new believers but for me as well. I remember one time in particular. Tent meetings were in progress, with many in attendance. One night, a drunkard staggered into the tent and began shouting for his wife. Finally spying her in the crowd, he pushed his way toward her. She ran from him and cowered at the feet of the pastor's wife. Before anybody could intervene, he kicked her viciously, then threatened to kill her if he found her at the tent again. Fortunately, in the heat of the argument, his wife managed to escape and fled into the city where he was unable to find her.

In any case, the stress of those months eventually caught up with me in November, about two months before Hilda's furlough. Tired and knowing that I would soon be left alone, I was particularly vulnerable and became both physically ill and emotionally depressed.

One day, I hit bottom. Fatigued, pressed by the enemy of my soul and in terrible physical pain, I cried out to God in frustration. "God, I can't take it any more. Please let me get pneumonia and die!" A week later I was burning with fever and had lost my voice—I had pneumonia.

The Lord began to deal with me and I sud-

denly realized my selfishness in wanting to
die when there were still so many souls in
darkness. I confessed my sin and asked God
for life. Almost immediately my fever and
chest pain began to subside, and the next day
I was able to preach and had the privilege of
leading several people to Christ. It was a day
of both physical and spiritual healing for me,
a day when I realized that every time a Japanese person gave his or her life to Jesus, the
joy I felt more than made up for any discomfort, illness or exhaustion in my life. With my
heart revived, I began to receive assurances
from God that many people would come to
know Him, that even a greater harvest was
yet to come.

When I first began my ministry in Matsue, I
made a rather strange request to God. The
area in and around the city of Matsue was
known for its idol worship and lack of receptiv-
ity toward the gospel. Missionaries before me
had preached their hearts out with few results.

One day I knelt before the Lord and asked
Him to bring the worst man in town to us. The
reason? I believed it would be a tremendous
testimony to the local people if they could witness someone's life dramatically changed before their eyes. As busy as I was, however, I
soon forgot about the prayer.

Then, about a year later, on one of those rare
occasions sitting in the living room enjoying a

quiet day to myself, I was startled by the sound of a greeting outside.

"*Gomen kudasai* (excuse me)." It was a man's voice.

A well-dressed Japanese gentleman stood at the entrance. Looking past him, I noticed a brand new bicycle leaning against the veranda.

"What can I do for you, sir?" I asked, bowing low.

"Is there a priest living here?" he inquired anxiously, bowing in return.

"No, I'm afraid not," I responded, "but my friend and I are missionaries. Can we help you?"

He fidgeted momentarily.

"What is God like?" he finally blurted out.

"Oh!" I exclaimed, thrilled by the question. "You have come to the right place! Please do come in!"

Showing the way into the living room, I directed him to our pint-sized couch. After he was seated, I pulled up a chair directly in front of him and opened my rather large Japanese Bible to the book of Genesis. Discovering that his name was Mr. Kodake, I then painstakingly worked my way through the pages. He listened intently, never once taking his eyes off me.

I explained to him how God created man in His own image in order to have a perfect relationship with him; how mankind was not satisfied with its relationship with God, disobeyed Him and fell into sin. Next, I explained how we were all sinners, incapable of a relationship with God in our present state. All the while, Mr. Kodake nodded, drinking in every word.

I continued to explain how sin had created a chasm between us and God, a chasm which only God could bridge. Then, turning to the Gospels, I began to outline how God bridged that gap through Jesus. Gently I told how God the Father sent His Son to pay the price for our sins on the cross, suffering a painful death in the process. I ended with the story of the resurrection. Through the entire narrative Mr. Kodake's eyes continued to bore into my soul. It was as if he didn't want to miss a single syllable.

Having completed my explanation, I tried to discern from the look on his face whether or not he understood. It appeared he did. So, saying a quick prayer, I continued.

"Wouldn't you like to ask forgiveness of your sins and receive Jesus as your Savior right here and now, Mr. Kodake?"

His face lit up.

"Oh! I knew there must be some provision made for man somewhere!" he exclaimed. Then, bursting into tears, he reached over and grabbed my hand. "Yes, Miss Dyck! I want to receive this Jesus!"

We bowed our heads. With words that could only be described as emotionally charged, he tearfully begged God for forgiveness. It was a moving moment for both of us. When he ended his prayer, I looked up. You should have seen his face. It was radiant, filled with relief and incredulous joy.

"Miss Dyck, I feel wonderful! You must help me to learn more of the Bible! I want you to spend every spare moment you have so I can study it with you."

Having many other duties to attend to, I nevertheless promised to spare him as much time as I could. So, whenever possible, we poured over the Scriptures together. Sometimes he would stay up to eight hours at a time. Intensely curious and hungry for God's Word, the more we studied, the more questions he had.

As I got to know Mr. Kodake better, I discovered that during the war he had been in the military as an airplane engineer. Arriving back home after the Japanese surrender, he started his own business. Unfortunately, because of the poor economic situation, there was little or no market for his product and he was forced to declare bankruptcy.

Eventually he introduced his children to me, but never his wife. I found that rather strange, so one day I asked if I could meet her. Gently, but somewhat mysteriously, he refused me. I didn't pursue the subject.

Soon after, though, I discovered why. Walking home from work in the late afternoon one day, my next door neighbor, a Mr. Owake, the top prosecuting attorney in the community, slid open his front door and called me over to chat for a moment. I could tell immediately that something was troubling him.

"That man Kodake," he said brusquely, "what does he want at your house all the time?"

Puzzled by his stern manner, I replied innocently, "Well, Mr. Owake, we're studying the Bible."

Now it was his turn to look puzzled.

"The Bible?" he asked, his voice dripping with skepticism.

"Yes," I said, nodding my head.

Unable to believe what he had just heard, he continued.

"Well, did you know that he might just cost you your life?" he added sternly.

"That's all right," I replied naively. "I'm going to teach him the gospel and if my life is taken because of that, well, that's just fine."

"You don't understand, Miss Dyck," Mr. Owake continued with even greater intensity. "I have come to warn you."

"Warn me about what?" I asked, perplexed.

"Kodake is the most dangerous and violent man in Matsue!"

I couldn't have been more shocked! However, as Mr. Owake proceeded to divulge an incredible story of violence and cruelty, I could see why he was so concerned.

Kodake was an alcoholic whose savage outbursts were often accompanied by the use of knives. Apparently, when on a drinking binge, he could lose control of his mental faculties as if some demons were in possession of him. Because of this, he had been in and out of prison since returning home from the war.

"I find that hard to believe!" I countered. "Mr. Kodake is such a courteous gentleman."

"Oh, when he's sober, you couldn't find a nicer man," Owake replied. "But you haven't seen or heard the worst of it yet."

The story he related was a gruesome tale. One night, after spending the entire evening with his drinking buddies at a local bar, he staggered home in a drunken stupor. At the door of his home, he glared belligerently at his wife. Being a quiet lady and continuously supportive, she made every attempt not to provoke him. But as the night wore on, he continued to drink heavily and, as he did, his rage steadily increased. Eventually he retrieved a huge butcher knife from the kitchen and began to threaten his wife with it.

Fearful for her life, she tried to calm him down, but to no avail. Finally, in a fit of rage, he lunged at her, shoving the knife into her thigh. In the frenzy that followed he slashed both legs, severing the tendons. As she lay on the floor, a pool of blood slowly forming around her, he glowered down at her. Then, as the sight of blood began to clear the fog from his mind, almost instantly his anger vanished and he sobered up.

Now his military training took over. Quickly

he took the belt from around his waist and made a tourniquet above the gaping wounds on his wife's legs. Then he bundled her up and rushed her to the hospital where he confessed what had happened. His wife was left partially crippled.

When the city officials got wind of what happened, they decided that this latest rampage was the last straw. In court he was informed that if he stepped out of line again he would be banished from the city, never to return. Now, that might seem like light punishment for such cruel and violent acts, but it must be remembered that things in Japan were still rather unsettled because of the war. To be thrown out of one's home could have serious repercussions.

In any case, his deeds and the threat of punishment had a profound effect on Kodake. Filled with remorse at what he had done to his wife, he found himself on my doorstep a few days after that tragic night. I thanked Mr. Owake for his warning, reassured him once again of Kodake's authentic conversion and then walked back to my house.

God indeed sent me the worst man in town! I thought to myself. *But He has also changed him forever!*

As the weeks and months went by, Hilda and I continued to work with Mr. Kodake. He, in turn, remained consistent in his studies, faithfully attending all church services and growing ever stronger in his Christian faith. I decided not to let on that I knew of his past, waiting instead for him to tell me himself.

It wasn't long before he began sharing his new-found faith with others. He brought some of his military friends and we had the privilege of leading a few of them to the Lord. One of them was Mr. Fujihara, an accountant.

Then, on Christmas Eve 1956, Mr. Kodake and his fourteen-year-old daughter paid me an unexpected visit. I could tell he was excited about something. After a moment or two, he informed me that he had learned about baptism from studying the Bible and now he wanted to be baptized. I explained that our pastor would be happy to baptize him, but that it would be better if he waited until spring when the water wasn't quite so cold.

"What has that to do with baptism?" he asked, a puzzled look on his face.

"Well, we baptize in Lake Shinji," I answered, equally puzzled.

"But, Miss Dyck," he countered, "didn't water baptism end with John the Baptist?"

"No, Mr. Kodake, it didn't," I replied. "But tell me, what is it that you want to be baptized with?"

"I want to be baptized with fire and the Holy Ghost like Jesus was," he said firmly.

How diligently he must have been reading his Bible to discover the beauty of being filled with the Holy Spirit, I thought to myself. I took a few moments to explain to him the importance of water baptism, then concluded by telling him that if he followed the Lord in water baptism it could very well be that he would receive the baptism of the Holy Spirit at the same time.

"I want to be baptized with both," he replied with determination.

We discussed an appropriate date. After some deliberation he chose the day of Pentecost, the same day that the disciples were filled with the Holy Spirit after Christ's ascension.

A word of explanation is needed here to help western readers understand the ramifications of Christian baptism for a converted Japanese. Most Japanese homes house a Shinto shrine which is often adorned with a bronze Buddha. If the family is wealthy, the Buddha might be gold-plated. Ancestral tablets are placed somewhere on the shrine and are used not only as a record of the family tree but also as the focus of their ancestral worship.

Although Mr. Kodake had become disillusioned with idol worship and had destroyed his idols long before his conversion, his dislike for them intensified after his decision to follow Christ. As a result, whenever someone came to know Christ, Mr. Kodake spent many long hours convincing that person of the folly of hanging onto their ancestral and idol worship.

As missionaries we did not encourage the destruction of their cultural heritage and always assisted new converts in preserving the names on their ancestral tree. However, we did ask them to destroy those things which could lead them away from the worship of God. Many gladly complied, experiencing freedom from a rigid, hopeless and futile religion that focused on the worship of dead ancestors and numerous wooden and stone gods rather than the living God.

Some Christians were unable to destroy their idols immediately, especially if the eldest member of the family was not a Christian. You see, in Japanese culture, the oldest living family member's wishes are always respected. So we encouraged new Christians to wait until their family member either came to know Christ or passed away before destroying the family idols.

It was quite a day when Mr. Kodake, his friend Mr. Fujihara and a few others followed the Lord in baptism in the waters of Lake Shinji—after they burned their idols, liquor bottles and anything else that might come between them and God.

That night, back in Matsue, we held a celebration service. Mr. Kodake testified that after his baptism he experienced a feeling deep inside comparable to waves crashing on the shore. At the time he had felt there must be some kind of significance to this and scurried home to search the Scriptures for an answer. He found it in the book of John: " 'Whoever believes in me, as the Scripture has said, streams of living water will flow from within him.' By this he meant the Spirit, whom those who believed in him were later to receive . . ." (John 7:38-39).

It was obvious, not only from Kodake's words, but also from his subsequent actions, that he experienced not only water baptism but also the filling of the Holy Spirit that day. Never again did he touch alcohol or bring a cigarette to his lips. He emerged as one of the first board members of our fledgling church and became involved in prison work. On behalf of the Alliance and the Gideons, he also distributed hundreds of Christian books and Bibles.

The most notable change in him, however, was in the way he treated his wife. He finally found the courage to tell me what he had done to her and, overcome with shame, eventually introduced me to her. Never did I see anyone more totally dedicated to the welfare of his spouse than Mr. Kodake. He treated her with tremendous love and respect.

Then one day, a precious event took place— Mrs. Kodake accepted Christ and asked to be baptized. Now their whole family, including their two children, were believers.

The day of her baptism we gathered once again on the shores of Lake Shinji. Kodake bent down and picked up his wife, holding her lovingly in his arms as she wrapped her arms around his neck. Then, cradling her gently, he slowly carried her into the water and stayed by her side as the minister baptized her. It was a picture of complete devotion, and it brought tears to my eyes.

Here was a man—the worst man in the city, one who had been controlled by rage and the liquor he consumed, a man who had cared only for himself—who had now been transformed through the blood of Jesus into a loving husband, father and man of God!

11

"Will God Pay My Debts?"

The day began much like any other. Awakening early, I made my way through the snow to the property we had recently purchased. It was an ideal piece of land just two blocks from my residence. On the site stood an old house which we were in the process of gutting.

I pitched in enthusiastically, tearing at the old lumber and clearing away the accumulating rubbish. In a relatively short time, beads of perspiration glistened on my forehead and I hardly noticed the cold air blowing through the building.

An hour or so later, I heard the crunch of footsteps on the snow. The door opened and two men entered. I called out a greeting to one of them, Mr. Kodake. His companion was a distinguished looking gentleman, obviously troubled. Putting down my tools, I walked over to them.

"Miss Dyck, I want you to meet an old friend of mine from our days in the military," Kodake began. "His name is Mr. Matsumoto."

Mr. Matsumoto bowed in greeting, but would not look me directly in the eye. After I returned his bow, Matsumoto suddenly became very serious.

"Miss Dyck," he said finally, "I am in considerable trouble, but I've heard how this Jesus Christ helped my good friend Kodake. I am wondering if maybe there is some help for me."

I glanced in the direction of the pastor who had just arrived but was already engrossed with his work. He didn't seem able to set aside what he was doing.

"Let's take a walk to my home, Mr. Matsumoto," I said finally. "We can talk there."

Back at my place I began sharing the gospel with this troubled man. At first he was attentive, then suddenly he leaned forward and put his head in his hands. Thinking he was tired and no longer wanting to listen, I said, "You seem very tired today, Mr. Matsumoto. Why don't I stop talking and you can come again tomorrow?"

"No, no!" he exclaimed, lifting his head momentarily. "Please continue!" What I didn't know at the time was that the story of God's love had brought back memories from his teenage days, more than thirty years before, when a famous missionary to that part of the country, Barkley Buxtom, had told him the same gospel story.

I forged ahead, explaining in detail God's plan of salvation and ending with these words: "If you will receive Jesus Christ as your Savior, Mr. Matsumoto, He will make you a brand new creation. Would you like to receive Him?"

He paused for a moment.

"If I take this Jesus as my Savior, will He pay all my financial debt?" he asked pointedly.

The question caught me off guard. With my mind swirling, I shot up a desperate prayer for wisdom. Suddenly, I was reminded of Jesus' words in Matthew: "There is no man that has left houses or lands for my sake and the gospel, but that he shall receive an hundredfold now in this time and in the world to come, eternal life" (19:29, my paraphrase).

Having heard what I perceived to be God's answer, I proceeded confidently.

"If you will take Jesus and follow Him with all your heart, and with all your soul and with all your might," I said, "then He will pay your debt and do even more than that."

"OK," he said. "I will receive Christ!"

With that we bowed our heads. I prayed and he prayed and then he began to share his story. As he did so, I couldn't help but feel a twinge of uncertainty inside. *Maybe I spoke too quickly in assuring him that his debts would be canceled,* I thought. You see, what he was telling me was far worse than I imagined.

Before the war, Mr. Matsumoto was a wealthy man, owning most of an island which was inhabited by about 6,000 people. There he built a large home and through the years became a very wealthy man.

When the Japanese military buildup began, he joined the army and became a high-ranking officer. However, by the conclusion of the war, his financial holdings, including a large portion of land, had been greatly diminished. On the verge of bankruptcy, he attempted to borrow some money to start a cotton batting factory in Matsue. Because of his excellent reputation, he was given the necessary loans. After starting the business, he moved his wife and three children into the city.

As the months dragged on he continued to lose money. Although there was a great demand for his product, few people had the cash to pay for it up front. As a result, a great deal of money was owed him. Eventually it became painfully apparent that he would be unable to collect most of it. And, with virtually no steady income, it became increasingly difficult to feed his family and pay back the bank. So he took to borrowing money from friends and business associates.

Before long, those who had lent him the money began demanding payment. Some of them eventually laid charges against him, hoping to recoup their losses through the courts. Ultimately, almost everything he owned was taken from him. He now had only a couple of small motorcycles left, a shell of his former business and what was at that time an astronomical debt of about $12,000. To make matters worse, his drinking and chain-smoking drained his finances even further.

When he concluded his story, as best I could I tried to reassure him in his newfound faith, encouraging him to place his trust in God. Then I gave him a New Testament and we said our goodbyes.

Over the next few days I spent many hours in prayer for Mr. Matsumoto and his family. In spite of his ever-increasing financial problems, he grew in his relationship with Christ and came to my place on several occasions to learn more about God and His Word.

One day he arrived while Mabel Francis was staying with me. She had come to see how the work in Matsue was progressing. When we were all seated in the living room, he once again directed the question to me that was most pressing on his mind: would Jesus really pay his debt?

I looked at Miss Francis for support. Finally she said, "Well, Mr. Matsumoto, you follow Him and let's see what Christ will do for you." She then led him through the Bible, pointing out verses on the assurance of salvation. It helped reaffirm his commitment to Christ and reassured him that God would see him through whatever lay ahead.

The days passed. Christmas came and went and we continued to work on the church renovations, looking ahead to the day when we would hold our first service there. Then, on the afternoon of New Year's Eve, Matsumoto once again appeared at my door, this time on foot, his motorcycles no longer in his possession. I could see that he was more troubled than usual.

Apparently there was a custom in Japan which required that a person try to clear up all debts and business dealings before the New Year. The purpose? To save face and to allow one to bring in the New Year with pride and joy.

Frustrated at his seeming inability to do what custom demanded, he ended his narration with a chilling comment. "Miss Dyck, if I don't get a large sum of money before the end of this day, I may as well not live. I just can't go on like this. One man has already threatened me. He has told me that if I don't give him a payment by midnight tonight there will be great trouble."

I knew all too well that the Japanese looked on suicide as the proper thing to do in situations like this. It was an acceptable way of saving face. So naturally I was worried at the tone of his comments. It was difficult to tell though if he was simply desperate or really contemplating the act.

"Our God is alive, Mr. Matsumoto," I began in earnest, not wanting to take any chances. "We need not fear. He is constantly near us. Let's get down on our knees right here and now and ask the Lord to send the money you need prior to the deadline."

Kneeling on my living room floor, we poured our souls out to God, asking Him to bring some much needed relief to my friend and his family. Following that, we continued talking until darkness settled over the city. It was late when he thanked me, then hurried down the street, hiding his face so none of his creditors would recognize or accost him.

The next morning, January 1, 1958, the city awoke to a light snowfall. Throughout the day I continued to pray for Mr. Matsumoto and his family, but I was restless. Fighting back the urge to visit him, I fidgeted at home, knowing that Japanese etiquette did not allow someone to impose on another on New Year's Day.

As the afternoon dragged on, the snow started falling heavily, swirling and drifting, building into a full-fledged storm. Then, around 5 p.m. I heard the unmistakable sounds of footsteps on the snow. *Who could be out on such a miserable day?* I wondered.

When I slid open the door, there was Mr. Matsumoto and his entire family covered in snow.

"We have something important to discuss with you, Miss Dyck!" Matsumoto began. "I know it's not proper to come on this day, but I couldn't wait. May we come in?"

I took their coats and motioned for them to be seated.

"Something amazing happened after I left your house last night, Miss Dyck," Matsumoto explained. "I was walking down the street hoping I wouldn't have to face anyone, when someone tapped me on the shoulder. I whirled around. As I did, a man spoke up. 'Where have you been, Matsumoto? I've been looking everywhere for you. I have come before the New Year to pay you the money I owe you.' He then placed a large sum of money in my hand and walked off." A huge smile lit up Matsumoto's face. He went on to tell me that the money was just enough to keep his creditors satisfied, at least for the time being.

"God answered our prayer, Miss Dyck!" There was a sense of awe in his voice. "I will never doubt Him again! Neither will my family! In fact, I want you to lead them to Christ! They are all in agreement!"

I looked at the rest of the family, each one eagerly nodding their assent. What a glorious sight it was to see them united in Christ that day!

Just before leaving, Matsumoto said he had a couple of favors to ask of me. When I inquired what they were, he said, "Well, first, my daughter has been taking sewing lessons, but our creditors came to the door not too long ago and confiscated our sewing machine. I was wondering if she could stay with you and continue working on her lessons at your place. She would love to help out around the house wherever you might need her."

"Oh, that would be wonderful!" I exclaimed.

He thanked me and bowed in appreciation.

"And the second favor?" I asked.

It was a rather strange request. He asked for some large sheets of writing paper, for some Bible verses that dealt with the evils of liquor and for the words to some hymns that explained the gospel.

Although puzzled at his request, I obliged, then watched as he began to write out each verse and song in beautiful Japanese characters. Apparently many of his friends would be coming over during the next five days expecting him to serve them liquor. He did not plan to do that and wanted to be able to explain why without offending them. He was hoping the poster-sized signs would help his friends understand. As it turned out, many of them respected him for his decision.

The New Year celebrations came and went and for a short time Matsumoto experienced some relief from the verbal bombardments of his creditors. However, they were soon back with a vengeance, troubling him even more

than before. Most distressing was their harass-
ment of his two young sons whom they tormented on their way home from school,
demanding that their father pay back what he
owed. Matsumoto began to fear for his family's
safety.

Before he could deal with that situation
though, he found himself entangled in a court
case. An elderly gentleman to whom he owed a
great deal of money was suing him. As the date
for his appearance drew near, he became increasingly worried. With virtually no money left
to pay his debts or feed his family, it seemed
more and more likely that prison would be his
fate. He diligently began to seek the Lord's will.

"When God speaks," Matsumoto asked, "will
I understand it in my head? Will I hear it with
my ears? Or will I know it in my chest?"

I reminded him that God's will was revealed
in the Bible. "If you pray to the Lord, Mr. Matsumoto, and read your Bible, He will surely reveal His will to you somehow," I responded.

On the day of his court case, he was up
around 3 a.m. strolling along the lakeshore
praying, as was his custom. Being the middle
of March, it was quite chilly, but with more important things on his mind, he was oblivious to
the cold wind that penetrated his clothes.

Two hours later he made his way back to his
family's modest apartment above a friend's
store near the waterfront. Slowly he trudged up
the long flight of stairs that ran up the side of

the building. Sitting on the tatami grass mat in the living room, he pulled his knees up and buried his face in his hands. Quietly he cried out to God, asking Him to somehow intervene.

"God," he finally prayed, "I don't care any more. If You want me to go through the embarrassment of a court case and prison, I will go. I ask only that Your name be glorified." It was an important step for him to take.

Sometime after 8 o'clock he heard the sound of footsteps climbing the stairs to his apartment. Suddenly, the front door slid open. An elderly gentleman stood wheezing and puffing in the entrance, trying to catch his breath.

"Be at peace, Mr. Matsumoto," he gasped. "I have called off the court case."

At the sound of the voice, Matsumoto looked up. The old gentleman continued.

"Here you are trying to make a home for your wife and your children and praying to your God. I know you've been suffering terribly, that your children have not had enough to eat. I'm calling off the court case." The man reached into his pocket. "Here, take this. Buy some food for your children and please forgive me for suing you." With that, he exited, sliding the door shut behind him.

Matsumoto sat in stunned silence, unable to believe his ears. Miraculously, one more hurdle was behind him. The Lord had provided once again!

Even though Matsumoto was now free from this particular court case, there was still much more that needed to be done before he was financially clear. So, in order to keep his family from being harassed further, he began to plan how he might best protect them. His brother-in-law had previously invited him to send his wife and children to Osaka until the problem was settled. Wanting desperately to know God's will, Matsumoto once again asked Him a simple question: should he keep his family with him or send them away?

The day before Easter found him up early in the morning, walking along the lakeside. This time, however, he became extremely cold within minutes. Making his way back to the house, he noiselessly entered the front door, careful not to wake his still sleeping family. Then, quietly, he cried to the Lord to reveal His will to him.

Suddenly, a voice said, "First Samuel 11!" Matsumoto was very frightened! This had never happened to him before. And besides, the phrase was foreign to him. However, he sensed it must be in the Bible. He opened his New Testament and searched the index. No Samuel!

"Lord, it's not here!" he cried out.

Wondering what to do next, he then remembered that I had also given him the entire Bible, a large cumbersome version which he had put on a shelf. He took the book and opened it to the index. Running his finger down the page, he came to First Samuel. With trembling hands, he found chapter 11 and began reading. He learned how King Saul had split his army into three parts and saved a city. What's more, it had all happened before the sun was high in the sky.

"I understand, Lord!" he said, thrilled at his discovery. "This can only mean that I must split my family into three, leaving my daughter at Miss Dyck's, while my wife and boys go to Osaka and I stay here." He also knew that there was only one train leaving for Osaka before the "sun rose high in the sky." The departure time was 8 a.m.

Matsumoto stood up, gathered his idols, tore down the shelf that housed them, along with his Shinto shrine and dumped everything into a large cardboard box. With that done, he again went down on his knees, put his face to the floor and worshiped the Lord, rejoicing in God's protective love and awesome power.

When his family awoke, he explained all that had happened. Pointing to the box, he said with confidence, "These gods are dead, but Christ is alive!" He had his wife and children pack their few remaining belongings and took them to the train station. Then he came straight to my house to tell his daughter and me what he had done and how he had arrived at the decision. What I saw was a man totally at peace with God.

The next morning was Easter Sunday. Many
people gathered for the service. Mr. Matsumoto arrived and sat at the back. Later, as the
pastor was about to give his message, Matsumoto called out. "Pastor, may I say something
before you speak?"

Mr. Matsumoto's face glowed as he walked
down the aisle.

"Today is Easter," he began. "If you want to
know if Christ is alive, ask me! I met Him yesterday morning! He's alive! He's awesome!
He's wonderful!" The words came tumbling out
of him as water rushes down a mountainside,
leaving in its wake a cool, refreshing spray.

"I have met the Lord face-to-face!" he continued. "I used to ask the pastor and Miss Dyck,
'How do you know when Christ speaks? Do
you know it in your head, your ears, your
chest? How do you know?' Well, I still don't
know whether it is in the head, ears or chest,
but this I do know—He speaks! I know Him. I
met Him yesterday. He's alive! He's in me,
above me, beneath me and on either side of
me! I am in Him and He is in me! Hallelujah!"

When he finished, there was hardly a dry eye
in the building.

After that wonderful day, Matsumoto fre-
quently dropped in to see me. Often he would
just sit on my couch, lower his head and commune with the Lord. Pointing at himself, he
would say to me, "He is right in this chest and
I can just talk to Him there."

Mr. Matsumoto, like Mr. Kodake, chose the day of Pentecost to be baptized. The day before that event, Mr. Kodake talked to him about the idols still stored in the box, how they must not be passed on to others in the family, but be destroyed.

"Yes, you are right, Kodake," he said. "They must be burned."

That Sunday afternoon found us all at the shores of Lake Shinji—the "Sea of Galilee" as we Christians called it. Besides the congregation, many of Matsumoto's unsaved friends were in attendance, probably to see what curse would befall him when he burned his idols.

Matsumoto was the last to arrive. Strapped to the back of his bike was a huge box. Everyone watched curiously as he dismounted at the shoreline and loosened the strings that held the box together. Then, lifting it up for all to see, he dumped the contents out on the sand—the Shinto shrine, the little bronze Buddha, still in it's small, gold-trimmed closet and a huge pile of black wooden tablets on which all the ancestors' names from centuries past were engraved.

Having witnessed Matsumoto's example, one by one the other baptismal candidates dumped their idols alongside his. As the kerosene poured over the dead gods, we began to sing hymns that spoke of the redemption and triumph that can be found in Jesus alone. Matsumoto's unsaved friends looked on quietly, fearing that at any moment bad luck would descend.

Then a match was thrown on the pile and soon the idols were engulfed in flames. As they burned, we sang hymns of victory. Then the baptismal candidates, including Matsumoto, plunged into the waves of the lake to be buried with Christ in the waters of baptism.

"I have gone with Christ through the events of the year," Matsumoto testified that evening. "At Christmas, the birth of Christ, I was born again. At New Years, the beginning of new things, my family and I started a new life together in Christ. At Easter, when Christ arose, I met the risen Lord. And tonight, at Pentecost, when the Holy Spirit was given to the disciples, I was filled with the Spirit as I came out of the waters of baptism."

It was Matsumoto's dream to have all his debt paid prior to his baptism, but he fell $200 short. However, the Lord blessed him and within weeks he was able to pay it off. Because of his testimony, some of his friends who had come to the lake to see if he would be cursed also received Christ.

Does God pay the debt of a man who is earnestly seeking him? I must admit, as this whole affair unfolded, there were times when I had my doubts. However, after witnessing an experience like this firsthand, all I could do was shout, "God, please forgive my doubting heart. Hallelujah! Glory to God and glory to the Lamb for sinners slain."

12

Prisoners Set Free

It was during the final year and a half of my first term that God opened the door to a rather unique opportunity in Matsue—a prison ministry. It all began when Kodake, Fujihara and I started working with their former military contacts, some of whom were struggling with alcoholism and the violence that often accompanies it. As these men came to know Christ and experienced freedom, our church soon developed a reputation that brought many hurting people to our doors.

One day, a young prostitute arrived at my front door. Because I was busy at the time, Kodake and Fujihara, who also happened to be there, took her to the church. She told them this rather bizarre and pathetic story.

The man she had been living with, a Mr. Fujioka, was in prison for theft. Separated from his wife and two children, and the only son of a wealthy and influential man in the city, he had been dragged down by his insatiable thirst for alcohol. The more liquor he consumed, the lower he stooped, until finally he was spending his entire weekly wage to satisfy his drinking habit. With virtually no money left over to feed or clothe the family, his wife was forced to take a part-time job. And through it all his father looked on in dismay, humiliated by his son's antics.

Finally, deep in debt with no one to extend him credit, Fujioka stole quietly one night into his home while his family slept. Taking his wife's expensive kimonos, he made his way down to the local pawn shop to obtain some drinking money. Now, there is nothing more precious to a Japanese woman than her kimonos. They are looked upon as family heirlooms.

The elderly Fujioka, unable to tolerate his son's shameful behavior any longer and fearing for the safety of his daughter-in-law and grandchildren, disowned his only son. He took the family to live with him, forbidding the younger Fujioka to have contact with his wife and children ever again.

With nowhere else to go, Fujioka eventually ended up with the young prostitute who now found herself at our door. With little or no income, he turned to thievery, even stealing from his friends. Finally, he landed in prison.

The young woman ended her story by asking if our church would obtain her lover's release.

Postponing the answer to that request, Kodake and Fujihara gently showed her how the lifestyle she had chosen was a sin and how dangerous it could be. Then they shared the love of Jesus Christ with her, explaining how she could experience forgiveness and begin a new life. They were able to lead this young lady to the Lord. Before she left, they assured her that they would try and make contact with Fujioka. And so our prison ministry began.

Kodake and Fujihara managed to obtain permission to see Fujioka. Miraculously, he too accepted Christ. Over the days that followed they began to disciple him, giving him a Bible and other literature to read. Eventually, he asked Kodake and Fujihara to attempt to seek his release, specifically begging them to urge his father to bail him out. Convinced that his conversion was genuine, the men broached the subject with his father.

"Mr. Fujioka," Kodake began, "your son has truly changed."

"I am not convinced of that," came the cold reply. "I believe my son has tricked you just as he has done others in the past. No! He is no longer my son! That's it!"

They continued to plead with the elderly Fujioka, but to no avail. However, they did not give up. During ensuing conversations and after a considerable amount of persuasion, their hard work and diligence paid off.

"I still do not want my son back," the father

said adamantly, "but if you can get the prosecutor to release him on bail and parole him, I
will pay his bail. However," he warned, "under
no circumstances will he be allowed to live here
in my house. I will not allow it! There has been
too much hurt already."

Kodake and Fujihara thanked the father for
his generosity. Determined to get the son out
of prison, they arranged a meeting with my
neighbor, Mr. Owake, the one who had initially warned me about Kodake. After some
deliberation, Owake admitted that it was too
big a decision to be made by him alone. However, he did promise to set up a meeting with
his fellow prosecutors for the purpose of con-
ducting a bail hearing. He ended the conversation by telling Kodake and Fujioka to prepare
their case.

Thanking him, the men left. Kodake toiled
many long hours preparing his arguments on behalf of Fujioka's appeal. Being an excellent or-
ganizer and a brilliant and well-educated man,
he was obviously the right person for the job.

Finally, the long-awaited day arrived. As Kodake walked into the hearing room he was met
by some influential lawyers, men he knew
would have to be thoroughly convinced before
they would let a man of Fujioka's reputation
out of prison.

For what seemed an eternity, they fired question after question in Kodake's direction.
Calmly he replied to them all until, ignited by

one particular question, his response changed
to fiery and fervent preaching.

"Mr. Kodake," one lawyer replied, "even if I
were to work on one prisoner for a lifetime, I
still might not be able to save him from himself. How can you suggest that this has been
done in Mr. Fujioka's case in such a short pe-
riod of time?

"You are right, sir!" Kodake fired back confidently. "No man can save another. Salvation
comes through Jesus Christ alone. It was Jesus
Christ who saved me and it is this same Jesus
who saved Fujioka. No one else."

The prosecutors excused themselves to delib-
erate the outcome. We waited anxiously, hoping and praying for a favorable decision. When
they returned some time later, one of them addressed Kodake.

"You have presented a good case," he said,
calling him by name. "Because of that, we have
decided that, if you can get Fujioka's father to
pay the bail, we will release him. But we will be
requesting a one-year probation. After that,
there will be another hearing."

What a relief! We all crowded around Kodake
to congratulate him. However, things were far
from over. Fujioka's father remained adamant
that he wanted no relationship with his son,
nor would he allow him to have any contact
with his family. To ensure that his wishes were
followed, he asked that Kodake and Fujihara
meet with his appointed liaison, Mr. Kajitani.

Together, the three of them were to work out the details regarding his son's release and future living arrangements.

The meeting was held in my home. I greeted Kajitani, Fujihara, Kodake and our pastor, then retired to my room to pray. As the meeting dragged on, I became intensely curious about the decisions being made in the next room. Eventually, needing to satisfy that curiosity, I decided to take them some refreshments.

I noticed immediately that something was not right. Although the other three men were carrying on a vigorous conversation, the pastor seemed very quiet. It wasn't long before I understood why. Mr. Kajitani indicated that Fujioka's father thought it best that his son live with the prostitute!

It took all the willpower I could muster not to speak up at that moment. As the discussion continued, I became increasingly disappointed when both Fujihara and Kodake reluctantly agreed to the plan. Kodake was chosen to approach the former prostitute to find out if she would take the younger Fujioka back. With that, the meeting broke up and everyone left.

All day my heart ached as I agonized over what I believed was an inappropriate decision. We had worked so hard to lead both these young people to Christ and to negotiate Fujioka's release. Now, we were about to throw it all away for the sake of convenience. In God's

Susan Dyck, during Bible school days, 1945-48.

The Henry Dyck family; Susan, far left, front row;
sister Betty, between their mother and father.

Canadian Bible Institute graduation class, 1948.
Susan, fourth from left, front row.

Burning idols before a baptismal service at Lake Shinji near Matsue.

Baptismal candidates prepare through Scripture reading and prayer.

Four people are baptized, including two businessmen Susan won to the Lord.

Susan identified these men as L to R: engineer, company agent and accountant. Although positive identification has not been possible, Mr. Kodake, left, was an engineer and Mr. Fujihara an accountant. Businessmen such as these were the ones Susan targeted for evangelism.

Susan and two university students with whom she held Bible classes.

Street meetings were a very effective means of evangelism in the 50s and 60s.

Field chairman, Paul McGarvey, with interpreter, Mr. Iguchi, and baptismal candidate. Mr. Iguchi was for many years a faithful assistant in the mission office.

Many Japanese children and young people reached by Susan
are in ministry today, including two Alliance pastors.

Youth rally sign identifies the group as being from
the Alliance Church in Yonago, about 35 miles from Matsue.

Susan embraces two girls from her young teen class.

Beautiful Mt. Daisan dominates the landscape near Matsue.

A tent meeting in Matsue. Susan's partner, Hilda Snider, third from left.

Susan preaches to a street crowd in Matsue area using sound system
mounted on the truck.

This picture is representative of fishing villages such as Shinji where Susan ministered. The tiny fish the woman is sorting are dried—head, tail and eyes—and used to flavor soups and other foods.

This typical scene shows grass-roofed homes and fresh-cut rice which is bundled and hung on racks to dry before being threshed.

Such an elaborate kimono could be worth up to $3,000 US today. Made of silk and worn only for special occasions, kimonos are often given to missionaries as gifts.

Of this picture, Susan wrote, "I'm happy when souls are being saved."

Mr. Matsumoto, owner of a cotton batting factory, and his wife pose in front of signs that read, "Matsue Bazaar, Limited Company, Ashahi . . . cotton . . . cotton."

A packed tent and overflow crowds hear the gospel message. The sign says, "God is Love. Special Evangelistic Meetings."

The Fujika family were good friends of Susan. Pastor Fujika often baptized those who were saved under Susan's ministry in Matsue (only pastors baptize). He is now the pastor of the largest Alliance Church in Japan, in Matsuyama.

Masako Sato commited herself to Christ so she could "get sparkling eyes and laugh like Miss Dyck."

The sanctuary and congregation of the Nagoya Alliance Church.

Anne Dievendorf, left, with Mabel Francis, Susan's co-worker and mentor.
It's "very Japanese" not to smile in pictures!

Susan Dyck, taken before she went to Japan in 1953.

eyes it was wrong! There was no use calling it anything else! That night, immensely saddened by the turn of events, I called out to God.

"Oh, Lord! What have we done? We've become mixed-up in something that will not bring glory to You. It will just be one big mess if we let this go on. Please help!"

Finally, two days later, during one of my prayer times, I sensed that God wanted me to do something about it. I began thinking of a way to approach Kodake without hurting his feelings. On the third day the Lord provided an opportunity when he arrived at my door.

"Kodake?" I began cautiously. "I have a special favor to ask of you."

"What is it?" he replied.

"Do you happen to know where the wife of Fujioka lives?"

"Of course I do!" he said, a puzzled look washing over his face. "It's no more than five minutes from here by bike."

"Would you let me meet her?" I persisted, hoping he would not think I was trying to take control of the situation.

There was a moment's hesitation.

"OK," he responded finally. He rode off on his bike and was soon back with her.

I could tell that Mrs. Fujioka was a little perplexed as to why she was being invited to visit the missionary lady. As yet no one had informed her of her husband's impending release. I began our time together with the usual small talk. But before long, an opportunity presented itself for me to share the gospel with her.

"Would you like to accept Jesus Christ as your Savior?" I asked as I concluded.

"Yes!" she replied emphatically. I led her through the sinner's prayer and proceeded to find out what had prompted her to respond so quickly. She informed me that her husband's sister had accepted Christ at a tent meeting in Matsue and had since been attending another Christian church. "Every morning she gets her fellow Christians at the bank where she works to pray for my husband," she continued. "She has also taught my children to pray as well. Because of that, every mealtime they bow their heads and pray that their father will change."

I was amazed at the goodness of God. Even though we had been trying desperately to appease Fujioka's father, God had other plans in mind. And, in spite of our fumbling, He had been preparing the groundwork. I decided to let her in on the secret.

"You know, Mrs. Fujioka," I said, hardly able to contain my excitement, "what happened to you today also happened to your husband not too long ago."

Now it was her turn to look shocked.

"It did?" she asked, tears glistening in her eyes.

"Yes, and we are on the brink of getting his

release. Your father-in-law has agreed to pay the bail. I invited you here today to ask if you would receive your husband back."

"Of course I will take him back!" she cried as the tears now streamed down her face.

What a great feeling to be part of God's plan that day! Later, when Kodake returned from escorting Mrs. Fujioka home, I asked if he had already approached the former prostitute about taking Fujioka back.

"No, Miss Dyck, I haven't," he replied. "I did not feel good about the manner in which we handled the situation. I also felt that perhaps Fujioka had not accepted Christ after all, that he was simply using us, as his father suggested. If that were the case, the repercussions would have been disastrous for us and the church."

On the day of his release, the men of our church escorted Mr. Fujioka from the prison to my home where his wife and children were anxiously awaiting his arrival. A bath had been prepared for him, along with dinner. When he and his wife met, they greeted one another reservedly, as befitting a Japanese couple in public. However, it wasn't too difficult to tell they were genuinely pleased to be together again.

As the weeks went by it was obvious to everyone that Fujioka's life had indeed been transformed. Whereas his only thought had been for himself, now he was industrious, disciplined and responsible. He remodeled his house and began working at Mr. Kajitani's bedding store as a salesman. His family started coming to church and he completely stopped drinking and smoking. No one could deny the transformation that God was working within this man. Eventually, the results were so dramatic that even his father began to take notice.

I made more trips to the prison. At first, Kodake always accompanied me, both because of my initial fear and the fact that unaccompanied women were not always welcome. Later though, as I became more comfortable, I made one to three trips monthly on my own.

One day, I was called to the prison by one of the inmates who had noticed my name on the inside cover of a Bible we had distributed. As I sat down across from him, a stenographer arrived and took a seat to one side. Evidently, with so many prisoners accepting Christ and then confessing their crimes, the prison officials thought it advantageous to provide a stenographer during my visits!

The first thing I tried to determine was whether or not this man had read one of our little books. When he nodded affirmatively, I then asked, "Did you understand what you read?"

"Yes," he replied quickly, "but there was one thing in particular that impressed me. That's why I called you." There was a slight pause.

Then, pointing at the booklet, he continued. "I read here that when Jesus was killed, two criminals were crucified beside Him."

I nodded. He continued.

"In the story, Jesus told one of them, 'Today you will be with me in paradise.' That impressed me a great deal. Would you tell me more about what this means?"

As I shared the good news of Jesus Christ with him, I watched his face closely, looking for any telltale signs that would indicate I was getting through to him. After a while, I noticed that the more I shared, the more excited he seemed to get. Finally, confident that his response would be favorable, I closed by inviting him to accept Christ as his Savior.

Immediately his expression changed.

"No, I can't," he said, hanging his head.

"Why not?" I countered.

He refused to answer. So I continued to probe, gently urging him to reveal the problem.

"I've killed someone!" he finally admitted. I waited for him to continue.

"I have never told anyone and I know if I do so now it'll make my sentence even longer than it is." Again he paused, wondering if he should continue. But now that he had started, it seemed he couldn't stop.

"I killed an elderly woman! It was after the war when no one possessed much of anything, especially money. My wife was a teacher, but with few government funds available to pay her, we were forced to borrow from an elderly woman just to get by."

He paused, the terrible anguish of his soul all the more visible.

"After some time, she began visiting us on occasion, constantly pestering us to pay her back. But we couldn't! There just wasn't any money. Finally, one day, after showing her into our house, I choked her in a fit of rage, took her into the garden, buried her and planted cabbages over the spot, hoping no one would suspect anything."

At this point in his story, he stopped once again, looking at me with deep, sorrowful eyes.

"Miss Dyck," he continued with a note of finality in his voice, "that woman never heard the gospel before she died. She never heard what I heard today. I have no right to accept Christ when the woman I killed never heard of Him nor had the opportunity to pray for forgiveness. After what I have done, to accept Christ would be a very selfish act."

The stenographer, who had been writing at a feverish pace, looked up.

"Listen to the lady," he urged the man. "Accept this Christ she is talking about."

The comment and the urgency of it surprised me. Although the stenographer himself had not accepted Christ as far as I knew, having heard the gospel countless times and having witnessed a number of dramatic conversions, he knew it worked.

"Listen," he began again, "you have 600 cell mates whom you can share this gospel with right here. You can tell them."

I could see a tremendous struggle taking place inside the prisoner, a battle of immense proportions, a battle between God and the devil, a battle for this man's soul.

Finally, God won! The prisoner sank to the floor on his knees, imploring God to forgive him and pleading with Christ to become his Savior. After a heart-wrenching prayer, he looked up at me.

"You know," he said, "up until now I have told only lies in court. If ever I am allowed to be free, I will walk this country back and forth telling people about Christ."

When his court date arrived, he stood before the judge, confessed his crimes and then preached a short sermon about what God had done for him. There was not a single dry eye in the courtroom.

The man was sentenced to Hiroshima Prison. But in 1980, he too was released.

Meanwhile, Fujioka and his family continued to follow the Lord. As his year of probation drew to a close, we all worked very hard to ensure his absolute release, especially Kodake, who had been chosen by the court to represent our congregation as a witness to the changed character of the former prisoner.

The long-awaited court date finally arrived!

13

Salvation in a Courtroom

The courtroom was jammed the day of the hearing. Relatives, friends and members of our church were there, some out of curiosity, others to lend their support.

The first witness to be called was the elderly Mr. Fujioka. As one of the prosecuting attorneys read off the long list of charges brought against the younger Fujioka, the father remained very still.

"What have you to say about all these charges concerning your son, Mr. Fujioka?" Mr. Owake finally asked.

"It is all true," began the father, tears unashamedly trickling down his face. "All these things are true. In fact, the half has not been told. From when he was but a little boy, this son of mine continually brought disgrace and shame upon our family. And up until last year he was nothing but a heartache and a trouble-maker." Then the old man's face brightened. "But last year all that began to change." Looking in the general direction of our congregation, he continued. "Because of that caring little church, their elders and the missionary, my son has become a new person. None of these charges are true any longer."

The tears continued to flow down his cheeks.

"Through the mercy of this Jesus Christ and the care of the people of the Alliance Church, he has truly been transformed. You don't know how grateful I am. He and his entire family now trust in this Christ and attend the church." He stopped for a moment and then added most dramatically, "And I want to say right here and now, in front of this entire courtroom—I vow that I and my whole family will become Christians as well."

By this time it was evident that God's Spirit was sweeping through the entire courtroom. Everywhere I looked people were weeping.

"I understand, Mr. Fujioka," the lawyer continued, "that your son has even given up liquor and tobacco. Is that correct?"

"Yes," replied the father proudly. "Due to the church, yes."

I glanced at the judge, his stoicism seemingly untouched by what he had heard. Then suddenly, a big tear escaped and began to roll slowly down his cheek. He pulled out a large

handkerchief from his robes and proceeded to
rub his forehead and around his glasses, as if
he was perspiring. Then, with an almost unde-
tectable gesture, he brushed his cheek to catch
the tear. I couldn't help but wonder if he too
knew what it was to have a wayward son.

Next, Kodake was called to the witness box.

"I understand, Mr. Kodake," began the
prosecutor, "that because of you and your little
church, this man, who was corrupt since childhood, has been made into a new person. Is that
correct?"

"I beg to differ, Mr. Owake," Kodake replied.
"I would like an opportunity to correct that
statement. No man or church can save anyone.
It is only through Jesus Christ and Him alone
that this man has been made a new person. Because of Jesus and the gospel He gave us, this
man has now been reunited with his wife and
family."

"Since his release from prison, what has he
been doing and what does he have planned for
the future?" Owake inquired.

"Well," Kodake responded, "at present, he is
working for Mr. Kajitani and looking after his
family. As for his future, he is seeking God's
will for his life. You see, we in The Christian
and Missionary Alliance believe the command-
ment of Jesus, 'Go into all the world and
preach the good news to all creation' (Mark
16:15). Beyond that, Mr. Fujioka has a right to
do as God directs him. But I can assure you,

whatever he does and wherever he goes, he will bear witness of God's saving grace in his own life."

That was Kodake for you—always looking for any opportunity to preach the gospel, even if the location was a packed courtroom.

Mr. Owake continued firing question after question at Kodake. When he was done, he excused the witness. Then, turning suddenly, he spontaneously addressed the audience.

"I want to tell all of you something," he said, choking back the tears. "I have lived next door to the missionary, Miss Dyck, who is here in the courtroom today. And over the months I have seen men and women such as Kodake come to her place for help. All were received graciously and helped immensely. But I have to admit that when the elders of this church to which she belongs came to me asking for the release of Fujioka because he had allegedly changed, I, along with the other prosecutors in this city were skeptical. We doubted that Christianity could have that kind of effect on anyone, especially a repeat offender. We allowed the one-year probation very reluctantly."

He paused to consider his words.

"But now I can honestly say that Fujioka has indeed been changed, and I can attribute this change only to the power of this Christ whom they worship. Because of this, I want everyone to know that from this moment on I will have confidence in the power of Christianity. I too want to receive this Jesus!" At that, he broke down, sobbing quietly.

With Mr. Owake weeping in the background, the judge, who had tried desperately to maintain his own composure throughout the proceedings, quickly rendered his verdict. "Based on the testimony we have heard today, Mr. Fujioka," he said, facing the young man, "you are free to go. This court is adjourned."

As soon as the judge left, the people from our church ran over to Mr. Owake, thanking him for his words and encouraging him in his decision to follow Christ. Unable to get to him right away, I joined in the celebration with the Fujiokas, their family and friends.

"Miss Dyck," the father said, "I want you to come to my restaurant for a celebration dinner to share in the joyous event that will see my son returned to his rightful place in the family."

What a beautiful feast awaited us! Calling for his son to stand beside him, the elderly Fujioka addressed the guests. At the conclusion of his speech, he took a piece of bread and gave it ceremoniously to his son. The younger Fujioka received it with the same reverence.

"Once I cut you off from the family," concluded the father, gazing intently at his son, "but now, in the presence of these witnesses, with the symbol of this bread, I receive you back into the family."

As I was trying to recover from this emotion-laden experience, Mr. Fujioka turned to me.

"And to you, Miss Dyck. From now on you are part of my family, like my very own daughter. The daily family bath will be prepared as always at 4 p.m. You are welcome to take advantage of this any time you please." (It was the custom in many Japanese homes to take daily afternoon soaking baths, like today's North American hot tubs. The practice involved a brief wash, then a soak in a large metal tub kept warm with a fire underneath, followed by another wash.) It was indeed an honor to be invited into that family tradition. However, being a rather shy Canadian, I took advantage of the offer only once.

Mr. Owake confirmed his commitment to Christ later that day. He also became like a father to me. But the rewards of that day were far from over. In addition to the miraculous conversions of Fujioka's father and Mr. Owake, Mr. Kajitani and his wife, a Mr. and Mrs. Hara and others in the Fujioka household were saved as well. All in all, about twelve people were eventually baptized in the waters of Lake Shinji as a result of that court case. God truly intervened in what had begun as a most tragic set of circumstances.

After six years in Japan, in April of 1959, I arrived home on furlough. One of the first things I was required to do was to fill out a medical form. The first three questions were as follows:

"Who is your doctor?"

Answer: "Jesus Christ!"

"Address?"

Answer: "He lives within."

"What have you done for worms?"

Answer: "Mark 16:18: 'When they drink deadly poison, it will not hurt them at all.' "

After filling out the yellow form and handing it in, I thought no more about it. However, as I was to discover later, other people thought a great deal more about it! At Alliance headquarters in New York City, it was decided that I was to have a complete medical checkup as soon as possible.

When Dr. Frame stepped into the examining room, I was surprised to see the yellow medical form in her hand.

"The first thing we are going to do is get rid of those worms," she said as she began an extensive medical examination. But at the conclusion, Dr. Frame shook her head in disbelief.

"Well, Susan," she said, "you are the first person from the Orient, whom I have examined, that never contracted worms."

And, in all my thirty-two years in Japan, I never did. Praise the Lord!

14

"You Will Walk Again!"

April, 1960, found me back in Japan for my second term. I was appointed to Shobara, a small inland city nestled high in the Chugoku Mountains of Hiroshima province. It was here, around the turn of the century, that the Alliance first began its work in Japan.

The thought of coming to this established center, with its numerous outstations sprinkled along the sometimes treacherous but beautiful mountain roads, awoke in me a spirit of adventure. I began to envision how God might use me during the next six years.

The pastor of the church in Shobara was a wonderful and dedicated elderly woman named Shizu Matsuyama. It was an absolute joy to work with her. However, the congregation was

another story. I soon discovered that the Shobara Alliance Church was in desperate need of
revival and cleansing. Having forgotten their
love of God, many had compromised their
faith in various ways. So I began to pray earnestly for revival. Not surprisingly, the Lord
made it clear that before doing a work in others, He wanted to do one in my own heart. I
complained bitterly to God, but He knew best.

Revival came in November of that first year.
Christians began confessing things long kept
hidden, such as adultery and alcohol abuse.
One woman, after reading A.B. Simpson's
book on the Holy Spirit, climbed to the second
floor of her home, got down on her knees and
told God she was not moving from the spot until she experienced the filling of the Holy
Spirit. Because of the way God touched her,
some of her family members came to know
Christ.

It was Easter Sunday, a day that turned out
to be much more significant to the work of
God in Shobara than we could predict. A number of us were walking to the lake for an open-
air service when we noticed some people
having a picnic. I stopped to invite them to the
lakeshore. They acknowledged the invitation,
but were noncommittal.

Unknown to us that day, one of the women
was impressed by the warmth and friendliness

of the offer and decided to contact me to discuss her troubles. However, before she had time to do that, she received news that her husband had boarded a train en route to nowhere in particular and had ingested some poison in an attempt to commit suicide. He had collapsed, they said, in a station down the line and had been rushed to the local hospital.

The wife found her husband drenched in blood but still alive. As she watched him lying in a semiconscious state, she became aware that her hands were still tightly clenched from the praying she had been doing on the way. God heard her desperate prayers, and four days later she was allowed to take her husband home. She, along with three friends, visited me and for several hours the four of them were on their knees weeping before Almighty God, confessing their sin and praising Him for His forgiveness.

But the story didn't end with their conversions. That was only the beginning.

One of the ladies told me that her nephew, a barber by trade, was "the worst kind of man, the most ill-behaved human being in town."

"Do you think that someone like him could ever be saved like we were today?" she asked. I assured her that nothing was impossible for the one true God.

The next day I received the shocking news that this woman had suffered a heart attack. Arriving at her home, I was led into the bedroom. Quietly I knelt beside her. Although vibrantly healthy the day before, she now looked extremely frail. I don't know how long I was on my knees, when suddenly I was startled by a voice directly behind me. It was the nephew, on his knees, repenting before God. I stared at him, unable to believe what my eyes were seeing. Then, before I knew what was happening, a messenger arrived to notify me that the man who had attempted suicide had been at my house with his wife.

I rushed to their home and found the wife crying. Her husband looked even more despondent than ever. In between her sobs, I was able to ascertain that around 4 that morning the doctor had informed them the poison had entered the man's brain and he was beyond help. Praying that God would speak hope and life to this dying man, I suddenly felt directed to read from Isaiah 53. When I came to the words, "Surely he took up our infirmities and carried our sorrows" (verse 4), they seemed to strike a positive chord in his tormented heart.

"Let me read," he said, picking up a Bible that lay beside him. He read the verse once, then a second time and a third. Then, clutching the Bible lovingly to his chest, he looked up at me, tears filling his eyes.

"This is it!" he exclaimed. "This is for me!"

I led him to Christ and concluded my prayer by asking the Lord to wipe the poison from his brain. Miraculously, God did just that! In one week he was back to work. Several months later, the man, his wife and three friends were baptized.

During my five years in Shobara, one other incident stands out. It involves a fifty-year-old Japanese woman named Mrs. Sito. Her story actually began five years prior to my arrival in Shobara. Evangelistic meetings were held in her small mountain village. Partially crippled, and for the most part bedridden for six years, she determined to attend even though it meant being transported piggyback style by a friend. She committed herself to Christ and then opened her home for weekly meetings which she conducted by crawling around on her hands and knees.

When I arrived in Shobara five years later, numerous Christians in the area came to me asking for prayer for physical healing. I noticed though that many of the older believers had not removed the idols in their homes. I told them about the verse in Exodus 23:24: "Do not bow down before their gods or worship them or follow their practices. You must demolish them and break their sacred stones to pieces." I told them that God would not remove their sicknesses until they had removed the idols.

One day, we received word that Mrs. Sito was very sick and was asking for someone to come and pray for her. Shizu, the elderly pastor, went because she knew I would refuse to pray for

healing if there were idols in the house. She discovered from Mrs. Sito that the only reason the
idols were still on her shelf was because she had
been unable to remove them due to her crippled
state. So Pastor Shizu took down the idols and
chopped them up with an ax. Then she prayed
and left. The next day we received word that
Mrs. Sito had been healed.

It was shortly after this that I visited her for
the first time. I found her praising God for her
deliverance despite the fact that she was still
having to crawl from room to room.

Moved at the pitiful sight of this sweet lady, I
put my hand on her knee.

"Mrs. Sito," I said, looking directly into her
eyes, "you will walk again!"

She reached down, exposing the stump of her
withered leg.

"With this leg?" she asked longingly. I didn't
know how to respond.

A few days later, exciting word came from
Mrs. Sito. Apparently, while meditating on the
book of Isaiah, she suddenly came to the reali-
zation that Jesus had indeed taken her sickness
on the cross in the same way He had taken her
sin. With that spark of hope filling her heart,
her eyes happened to focus on some tacks that
were lying on the floor.

Without giving it a thought, she got up and
walked over to the tacks. About to bend down
and pick them up, she stopped short! Looking
down at her feet, then back to where she had

come from, she suddenly realized that for the first time in many years she was walking! Excited beyond words, she strode around the room, thrilled at her newfound freedom.

It wasn't long before word of her healing spread throughout the entire village. One by one people came to see what this God Mrs. Sito claimed to serve had done. Grasping the opportunity, she told each of them the same thing, "Jesus has taken away my sin and because of that I am no longer a sinner. But not only that, He has also taken away my sickness."

Although her one leg remained shorter than the other, the twisted bones in her hand, arm and leg straightened out. Sometimes she could be seen walking for miles just for the privilege of telling the gospel story to yet another person. What a testimony she was to the life-changing power of a merciful and loving God.

Out of gratitude to her loving Father, she gave her property to be used for a church. We remodeled her house, built an additional two rooms for her use and utilized the main part of the building for the sanctuary.

Five years after our first meeting, Mrs. Sito suffered a stroke. Many times I made the long trip over icy mountain trails to care for her and the work she loved so much. It was indeed a sad day when God called this faithful servant home. However, her house became a lasting memorial to her and to God's miracle-working power.

15

More Miracles in Shobara

It was during my first furlough, prior to coming to Shobara, that God impressed upon me again a passage found in Mark 16. Jesus was speaking to His disciples after the resurrection: ". . . these signs will accompany those who believe: In my name . . . they will place their hands on sick people, and they will get well" (16:17-18). As you've already witnessed, God allowed me to experience the reality of those verses on a number of occasions.

Another such incident took place when our pastor was out of town. A lady from the church brought a friend to my place, a woman named Mrs. Mikami. She had an incurable liver disease.

During our conversation, I showed her a verse from Matthew. It spoke of Jesus as the one who "took up our infirmities and carried our diseases" (8:17). I explained to her that if we look to Christ for our salvation, then we can look to Him for our sicknesses as well.

"Do you believe in Jesus Christ?" I asked.

"No," she replied, "but tell me more about Him so I can believe." It was an invitation I couldn't pass up. I watched with delight as she bowed her head and accepted Christ as her Savior.

A knock at the door interrupted our conversation and Mrs. Mikami left before we could pray for her healing. The following Sunday night she came to church.

"Oh, Miss Dyck! Miss Dyck!"

I turned around at the sound of my name.

"Miss Dyck," she continued, her face radiant. "The other day when I was at your house I was so excited about receiving Christ as my Savior that I hurried home without asking you to pray for my liver."

"Yes, that's right," I replied. "Well, don't worry, Mrs. Mikami. There are some elders here. Let me find them and then we'll pray for you." Together we laid hands on this dear lady, as instructed in the book of James, and prayed for her.

She thanked us profusely and rushed home to tell her husband that her liver was healed. The following Sunday, Mrs. Mikami's husband appeared at church with her. He was genuinely delighted at what had transpired and had come to see for himself what this Christianity was all about.

In the meantime, our pastor returned from her tour. When she saw Mr. Mikami in church the following Sunday, she took me aside.

"Mikami Sensei is a very important man, Miss Dyck." I knew that the term *Sensei* was reserved for highly respected people. She went on to explain that he was the superintendent of education for the district and a member of the city council. The previous year he had also run for mayor but had been narrowly defeated.

The weeks went by. Mikami Sensei and his wife continued to attend our services. Then one evening after the service, Mrs. Mikami approached our pastor.

"Excuse me, Pastor," she began, "but, don't you have to be baptized to become a real Christian?"

Mrs. Matsuyama mentioned that she would be holding a baptismal service at the river the following Sunday. She also indicated that if the Mikamis wanted to be included, she would meet with them later in the week. Both responded affirmatively.

Not knowing what had transpired, I received a call asking me to pray for our pastor. The doctor had ordered her to stay in bed because of her increasingly poor health. When I arrived at her bedside, this godly but frail woman informed me of the baptismal plans, including the possibility that the Mikamis would be among those baptized. She was determined to go ahead with it despite her illness.

"But Pastor, Mr. Mikami is not even a Christian!" I exclaimed.

"I know," came her weak reply, "but the fact that he wants to be baptized means he wants to be saved." She paused briefly before continuing feebly. "I had every intention of going over to their home with their applications for baptism to prepare him for Sunday. But now, here I lie, too sick to go."

"Don't worry, Mrs. Matsuyama," I assured her. "If you will give me permission, I will visit them. Maybe God will give me the privilege of leading Mr. Mikami to Christ."

The next day I arrived at the Mikamis' second floor apartment. As was the custom, I greeted them from the bottom of the stairs. After a moment or two, Mrs. Mikami arrived at the top of steps and came down to meet me.

Bowing courteously, I said, "I brought your applications for baptism."

"Oh, we . . . uh . . . are not ready for baptism. We haven't even told our son yet," she stammered. Her hesitancy seemed strange in light of her previous enthusiasm. Not knowing quite how to proceed, I probed gently.

"Well, let's just forget about baptism for the time being, shall we? May I come up and talk with you and your husband about salvation?"

"No!" she whispered tersely. "It does not suit us tonight, Miss Dyck! Please come another time." She punctuated her invitation with a curt but polite bow.

It seemed obvious that Mrs. Mikami was desperately trying to hide something from me. But, with no other avenue open to me, I turned to leave. Then another voice called out, "Have Miss Dyck come up." It was Mr. Mikami.

Reluctantly his wife escorted me to their apartment. Mr. Mikami was seated at the end of a low table, a large Bible open in front of him.

"Hello, Mikami Sensei," I said, greeting him with a bow. He returned the courtesy. I glanced about the room. Nothing seemed out of the ordinary. I seated myself on the floor across the table from him.

"I was wondering if we could temporarily leave the subject of baptism, Mr. Mikami, so that I could speak to you about salvation and Christ?" He agreed. During the ensuing conversation he asked many questions. In answering them, I recounted an experience that had happened the night before. I had been up most of the night dealing with a lady who was obviously demon possessed. I told him how the demons began manifesting themselves whenever we started reading the Bible. Mr. Mikami listened intently.

"What causes people to become demon possessed?" he finally asked, leaning forward. I knew I had hit a spiritual nerve.

"Well, Mr. Mikami," I continued, choosing my words carefully, "there are many things that can cause demon possession. Fortune-telling, witchcraft, the occult and seances certainly provide an opening for such occurrences."

"Is there something about this in the Bible?" he asked, picking up the book in front of him.

I directed him to Deuteronomy 18 and asked him to read verses 10 and 11:

Let no one be found among you who sacrifices his son or daughter in the fire, who practices divination or sorcery, interprets omens, engages in witchcraft, or casts spells, or who is a medium or spiritist or who consults the dead.

His face turned pale. Mikami's wife nudged him and whispered something into his ear. I was puzzled. Later, I learned that when I arrived at the bottom of the stairs, he had been busy practicing his witchcraft. After hearing what Deuteronomy said about it, Mrs. Mikami had whispered to her husband, "And here you were doing those things."

"Let's get back to salvation," I persisted. "If you will take Jesus Christ as your Savior tonight, Mr. Mikami, He will make you a brand new creation."

Immediately the man bowed his head and directed a sincere and beautiful prayer toward heaven, asking Jesus to come into his heart. Then, in response to his request for baptism, I turned to Romans chapter 6. My hands were trembling. I couldn't help but marvel at the convicting power of the Holy Spirit. Carefully I explained how baptism is a symbol representing our identification with Christ's death and resurrection. I told him how, in Christ's death, we are drawn under the water, and then, as we come up out of the water, we are raised with Him to walk in newness of life.

"I think I understand it," he said, a note of anxiety in his voice. "When do I need to return this application?"

"Anytime between now and Sunday," I replied.

"Fine. I will bring them in tomorrow on the way to the office."

Following his baptism the next Sunday evening, Mikami Sensei gave the following testimony.

"I found what I have been searching for these last twenty years," he began. "Over the previous two decades I purchased some of the sacred scriptures of the world, reading them carefully. Then, a year ago, I made my way over to the cultural center and bought a copy of the Bible. I read it from cover to cover and came to the conclusion that, like the rest of the religious writings, it was a good book. However, I failed to see its significance for me at the time."

He paused briefly, then continued.

"One day, my wife came home and told me how she had found the Christ of the Bible. I began to feel that perhaps my search was ending. Then, earlier this week, Miss Dyck arrived at our house. She explained how to be saved and what baptism meant. I must admit that when she first told me about baptism, I didn't quite understand its symbolism. But she explained that it involved dying with Christ and then being raised with Him to walk in newness of life. At the time, I thought it was a literal death she was talking about. However, I had every confidence in the integrity of her words and trusted that I would be raised again should I die. So I went through with the baptism. What a wonderful feeling it was to be let down so gently under the water. Its meaning will always be special to me."

In the weeks that followed, Mr. Mikami's spiritual growth was phenomenal. Within a few months he became the top elder in the church. Little did he or we know what else God had in store for him.

It all began when the mayor of Shobara resigned quite suddenly. Mr. Mikami was asked to be the mayor.

"Gentlemen," he told the council committee, "I am not the man I was when I first ran for mayor. I have become a Christian since then and now God runs my life. I live according to the Bible and do not believe any man can live right without that book always at hand."

"We knew that something had happened to

you, Mikami Sensei," one of them responded. "But we still believe you are the only one who can lead this city." The entire committee nodded their assent.

"I'll tell you what, gentlemen," Mikami continued. "Open the mayoralty position to all who will let their names stand. If no one comes forward, then, being under the rule of Christ, I will take up my cross and shoulder this very important responsibility."

They did as he requested. No one came forward.

One month later the committee showed up at his front door with newspaper reporters and photographers. Then, piling into several cars, they escorted him downtown where they pronounced Mikami Sensei "Mayor of Shobara." At the conclusion of the ceremonies, they requested that he take them to the church where, for the benefit of the media, they asked him to stand behind the pulpit with his Bible so pictures could be taken.

"Lift that black book higher," someone shouted. "We want to see it." He obliged and the cameras flashed.

The next day, the various newspaper headlines boldly declared, "A Christian Mayor!" "A Bible-Teaching Mayor!" "A mayor that says, 'You can't live right unless you have the Bible always at hand.' "

During the eight years Mikami Sensei was mayor of Shobara, the city flourished. Beyond that, he made a huge impact for Christ, including the evangelization and conversion of some of his fellow council members.

One life—an influential life—rescued from witchcraft to serve the living God.

16

"Jesus Came into This Chest"

It was during my fifth year in Shobara that the field director invited me to minister once a month in an outlying village called Tojo, an hour and a half further up the mountain. The director had jokingly concluded our conversation with these words: "You like to minister to important men, Susan. Why don't you lead that wealthy man who lives up there in Tojo to the Lord?"

Instantly my ears perked up.

"Who is he?" I asked, my heart already starting to beat faster. "Tell me more about him and I'll sure try."

"His name is Yamamoto," he began. "He's president of a rather large company and has been called the richest man in Hiroshima Ken." He went on to explain that Yamamoto was the one responsible for building the church in Tojo although he never attended himself. His wife, however, was a faithful member.

I began making the monthly three-hour journey to and from Tojo and finally managed to get myself invited to the Yamamoto home. Although nothing special happened on that occasion, I did however get a chance to pray that Mr. Yamamoto would find relief from a physical ailment.

My next contact came on one of my regular monthly visits. The pastor of the Tojo church informed me of Yamamoto's decision to donate a very expensive chime set to the church. The pastor was thrilled and planned to hold a dedication service for the chimes. He suggested that we invite Miss Francis to be our special guest. At that time, she was close to retirement. After hearing that Mabel and I would both be attending the service, Yamamoto invited us to spend the night at his beautiful home.

Miss Francis arrived in Shobara Friday evening and stayed with me that night. Before leaving for Yamamoto's residence the next morning, I asked her for a favor.

"Miss Francis," I began, "I respect the way you trust the Lord. Would you claim Isaiah 61:1-3 with me? I want to ask God to use us in bringing the gospel to Mr. Yamamoto."

"Of course, Susan," Miss Francis replied. "I

would love to." We opened the Bible to that passage and laid hands on it, asking God to work through us by His Spirit.

After a slow and winding trip up the mountain road, we arrived in front of the Yamamoto residence around 3 p.m. The gate to the yard was wide open and there, standing on the veranda awaiting our arrival was this influential company president!

No sooner had the car come to a stop than he called for his servants.

"Take their car, service it and then put it away. They won't need it for a while."

Dinner that evening was served in the dining room around a low table. A legless, but delicately upholstered chair was provided for Miss Francis. With dinner over, we were informed that our bath was ready. Following the bath, we were directed to our bedroom where special foam mattresses and the best in wool blankets had been ordered for the occasion. Before leaving us for the night, Mr. Yamamoto pointed to the blankets and said, "Miss Francis, these are a gift from me to you. Please take them with you to the United States." With that he bowed and closed the sliding paper door behind him.

Later that evening, I turned to Mabel.

"Breakfast is at 8 o'clock. Why don't we take the opportunity to talk to Mr. Yamamoto about salvation before the service?" As usual, I was impatient, chomping at the bit like a horse anxious to run. I wasn't nicknamed "Bulldozer" for nothing!

Morning saw just the three of us seated at the table. At what I thought was an appropriate time, I leaned over and whispered, "Miss Francis, ask him what prompted him to give that expensive chime set to the church."

"Mr. Yamamoto," Mabel said, "if you don't mind me asking, what prompted you to donate the chimes to the church?"

Tears suddenly came to his eyes.

"There are so many boys making trouble in this town," he responded sorrowfully. "It is my hope that they will hear the music those beautiful chimes create, be drawn to church and hopefully change their ways."

The meal continued and all the while I was looking for another opportunity to speak to our host about spiritual things. Miss Francis seemed entirely oblivious to my impatience.

"Miss Francis, tell him that he too must be saved," I whispered when Mr. Yamamoto's attention was momentarily directed elsewhere. However, she made no move to guide the conversation in that direction. Finally, I could keep quiet no longer.

"Excuse me, President Yamamoto!" I blurted. "Why don't you receive Jesus Christ as your Savior? Then you could really help those boys."

Looking back on it now, I can't believe I had the nerve to barge in like that, especially with

Miss Francis there. I respected her ability and trusted her judgment in such matters a great deal more than I did my own.

Yamamoto paused, then slowly he reached under the table and pulled out an enormous Bible.

"I bought this a year ago," he began, his brow furrowed with concern. "I have tried to read it, but I can't understand a word of it. It is my hope that the town boys might better be able to understand it than me."

I was trying to think of a response to his comment when an idea suddenly came to me.

"President Yamamoto, it isn't so difficult to understand," I began. "Yesterday when we arrived both the front gate and the door to your house were wide open in anticipation of our coming. And there you were standing on the front steps to greet us. When you invited us in, giving us such a warm welcome and serving us that scrumptious dinner, well, it made us feel very special, very warm inside."

I paused for a moment, hoping my words would sink in.

"There's a verse in the Bible where Jesus said, 'Here I am! I stand at the door and knock. If anyone hears my voice and opens the door, I will come in and eat with him, and he with me' (Revelation 3:20). Mr. Yamamoto," I persisted, "if you would do for Jesus what you did for us, if you would say, 'Jesus, my heart's door is open. I want You to come in,' then He will come in. It's as simple as that."

"Well, I could do that," he replied, a glimmer of understanding in his eyes.

Since I always enjoyed hearing Miss Francis pray, I asked her to say a prayer and lead this man to Christ. However, no sooner had she begun with a sentence or two, than Yamamoto interrupted.

"Jesus, my heart's door is open!" he cried. "I want You to come in right now!"

Miss Francis got up and moved to his side. In the minutes that followed she told him the story of the prodigal son, how, when he returned home, his father ran out to meet him and received him back. I went to kneel beside him too.

"Miss Dyck," he said. "I do understand! The Father has received me and Jesus has now come into this chest." He gave his breast a thump for emphasis.

As I stood to my feet, the sliding door opened and in walked Mr. Yamamoto's son, the vice-president of the company. This time it was Mabel's turn to prod me.

"Speak to him too, Susan," she whispered.

Without a moment's hesitation, I turned and bowed. He reciprocated.

"Your father has just received Jesus Christ as his Savior," I began, getting right to the point. "Wouldn't you like to do the same thing? After all," I concluded, "you could then serve the Lord together."

I waited with bated breath, watching to see

how he would respond to such a direct approach. To my total surprise he said, "Actually,
that's why I walked in. I was on the other side
of these paper doors and heard everything."

Again we bowed our heads and prayed the
sinner's prayer. I heard a rustling sound behind
me. Looking up, I saw the pastor of the Tojo
church. He had entered the room and knelt beside us.

"Pastor, the president and his son have just
received Christ!" I shouted.

The pastor greeted them warmly, then turned
toward me.

"Miss Dyck," he said, "the president of the
Hiroshima Bank has injured his back. He
would greatly appreciate it if you could come
and pray for him."

"Is he a Christian?" I asked.

"No, he isn't," the pastor replied, "but his
wife is. They live just behind the church."

The elderly Yamamoto called his servants to
bring our car around. In moments, the three of
us, Miss Francis, the pastor and I, were on the
road.

We found the bank president propped up at
a low table, obviously in a great deal of pain. I
gently brought the conversation around to his
spiritual well-being.

"If you will look to the cross, sir, and receive
Jesus Christ as your Savior, then we will look to
the cross for your healing. If it's alright with

you, Miss Francis will pray, and then lead you to Christ."

"Oh, I don't quite think I am ready for that yet," he responded.

"Well, let's just pray and see what happens," I said finally.

Miss Francis prayed a brief but pointed prayer. No sooner had she said "amen" than the man started to pray on his own, a truly repentant cry to the Lord. As he concluded, the three of us rallied around him, laid hands on his back and prayed for his healing. Since the service was about to start, we left without knowing the results.

Arriving at the church, I noticed that Mr. Yamamoto, his wife and his son were already seated in the front row. As I took my seat I happened to glance at the door. My jaw dropped! The bank president, standing tall and straight, was walking in with no hint of back trouble whatsoever. He had been completely healed!

With the church filled to capacity, Miss Francis preached. Then, at 1 o'clock, the dedication of the chime set took place. After several speeches, Miss Francis preached another simple but powerful message. Some men who had never been at the church before were very impressed.

The evening service was more informal, with opportunity for people to give testimony of what God had done in their lives. Instantly, a businessman who had been at the dedication of the chimes jumped up.

"This afternoon I heard Miss Francis speak and I decided that I would become a Christian as soon as I got home. But as my wife and I were traveling, I suddenly sensed that I shouldn't wait. So, pulling the truck to the side of the road, I said to my wife, 'I don't know what you would like to do, but I want to kneel right here in this truck and receive this Christ the lady was talking about.' " They accepted Christ together, and before the sun had set, Mr. Yamamoto's daughter-in-law also accepted Christ. What an exciting day!

When people stopped him on the street and asked, "How is it that you have changed so much, Yamamoto Sensei?" he would put his hands on his chest, tears would fill his eyes and he would reply, "It's all because Jesus came into this chest."

With each new person that came to the Lord in Shobara, I would reflect on one verse: " 'Not by might nor by power, but by my Spirit,' says the LORD Almighty" (Zechariah 4:6).

It was so true!

17

To Humble You and to Prove You

In the final year of my second term (spring of 1965), I unexpectedly received a call to return to the church in Matsue. The Matsue church, I found out, was in a sad state of affairs. Except for the Sunday morning services, all meetings had been discontinued, including those at two outstations, Mitsu and Shinji.

I was encouraged by the dedication of Pastor Fujika and his wife. With tears they shared their belief that they had failed God in their ministry and asked for my input and help. I extended my love and encouragement to them, promising that together we would turn the situation around.

We met for prayer to determine God's will, then drew up plans for rebuilding the work.

The plans included reinstating the midweek prayer meeting, an early morning worker's prayer time and Sunday night evangelistic services. As soon as possible we also reopened both children's and adult services at the two outstations.

I began visiting the believers who had strayed away. All the families but one were back in the fold within a few months, zealously following the Lord once again, some even bringing their tithes up to date.

Just one year later, my second term came to an end and I found myself homeward bound once again. However, knowing that I would be returning to Matsue for my third term made the year go by quickly. I couldn't wait to get back.

On April 13, 1967, I returned to Japan, the country that had become my first love, my real home. The lovely Baptist Mission house I had resided in a year earlier was again at my disposal. As I pulled up to the door that first day, however, I was shocked. The once-beautiful dwelling was in obvious disrepair. The inside was no better. The rain had leaked through the roof, damaging ceilings and floors. The bathroom fixtures were coated with rust and, while checking the attic, I stumbled upon a huge snake skin, no doubt shed by a rather large reptile!

Back on the porch, I gazed out at what had

once been a beautiful lawn. It was overgrown with weeds and tall grass. Thinking of the snake skin in the attic, I couldn't help but wonder if the grass might not be infested with an assortment of slithering creatures. Before I could brood too long over the state of affairs though, the pastor and some of the believers from the Matsue church appeared with scrub pails in tow. Before long, the dilapidated house had been changed into comfortable living quarters and the yard retrieved from the call of the wild.

During the early part of January, I had a wonderful experience with the Lord in my quiet time. It was right out of Isaiah chapter 6. I saw the Lord high and lifted up in all His glory. Then a great vision of a coming revival came to me and I felt heat applied to my lips.

"Lord," I asked, "what is the meaning of this?"

"Lo, this hath touched thy lips, and thine iniquity is taken away and thy lips purged to proclaim the truth in this revival," came His reply (6:7, my translation).

In the days that followed, the Lord continued to come to me with revelations of Himself and the coming revival. It was indeed a wonderful experience. However, I once again faced the mundane chore of moving. The Baptist house had been sold.

I discovered that there were houses available on the south side of the city, but for some rea-

son I sensed a firm conviction that God was
going to provide a home for me on the mountain in the north. As moving day drew near, I
was no closer to finding a place than the day I
began my search. In fact, when the last day of
January arrived, I called the movers to load my
belongings, but gave them no forwarding address. An hour before the trucks were scheduled to arrive, a friend stopped by. She lived in
a brand new residential area on the north side
of the city. Apparently, one of the families who
had built a house in that district had been
transferred and the house was vacant.

We piled into her car and drove to the house.
Although we were unable to see the inside, I
knew it would be more than adequate for my
needs. When we finally located the owner, he
agreed to rent the place to me, at least temporarily.

I arrived back at my old house just as the
truckers had finished loading my belongings. I
climbed into my car and led them to my new
quarters! I had no idea why God wanted me
there but it wasn't long before I found out that
there were 200 homes in the subdivision, all of
them built within the previous year. Most of
the residents were families of government
workers or policemen. What a great opportunity!

Even before I was completely settled in, in
true Japanese fashion I went around to call on
my immediate neighbors. Although it was also

the custom to bring along a small gift when one went calling—like a box of matches, a bar of soap, a towel or some cakes—this being only my temporary residence, I didn't feel it would be necessary. However, I did take along some tracts and pictures of our church with its address. The women were very friendly and gladly accepted the literature. Three of them insisted that I come in for a cup of tea.

In the days that followed, one lady offered me the use of her telephone. Someone else offered to store my extra tires in his garage and his wife often took my clothes in off the line when it started to rain. Yet another neighbor built a concrete garage for me, insisting that it was not good to leave my car outside.

I soon discovered that there were deep spiritual needs. One particular lady said, "I have been longing to go to a Christian church and really didn't want to go alone. I had no one to go with until now."

Another woman said, "Twice before I have come in contact with Christians and have done nothing about it. I feel this is my last chance. I'm glad you're here." And with each new introduction, my amazement grew. I could never have imagined this kind of spiritual readiness in Japan. The vision I had back in January began to make more sense when a number of women accepted Christ as their Savior and came with me to the Sunday evening services.

Because the house on the mountain was only my temporary residence, it was imperative that I begin looking for more permanent accommodations. With a sad heart I realized that what I might gain in permanency, I would definitely lose in other ways, especially when I considered the intimate friendships I had established with my neighbors.

Fortunately, I didn't have to wait long. One of the believers in the church owned a piece of land near the church and offered to build a house to my specifications. It was a real answer to prayer. With only a couple of days left in November, I moved in, just beating the onslaught of winter and the busyness of the Christmas season. I had insisted that the living room be large enough to accommodate my Bible classes and women's meetings. When twenty-three women gathered at my place a week before Christmas and another nineteen on the 23rd of December, I felt that my work on the house had been worth the effort.

Early in the new year, though, disaster struck. After the New Year's service, I invited the young people and the pastor and his wife to my home for a snack. We sang around the piano and generally had a lot of fun. When the young people left shortly after dark, the pastor, his wife and I proceeded to the kitchen to prepare a light meal.

Suddenly, without warning, there were two small blasts, followed quickly by a loud explosion! The building shook. We looked at each other. It seemed like the explosions had come from the living room. Instinctively, all three of us made our way to the source of the blast. I pushed the door open gradually and peeked inside. I couldn't see a thing! The room was filled with black soot so thick that the lights were virtually invisible. I shoved the door further and walked into the room. Thick smoke was pouring out of the stovepipe that now hung loosely to one side. Instinctively, I glanced about the room, searching for the other pieces that were normally attached to the stove. They had blown across the room and landed near the door leading into the kitchen. How fortunate we were that we walked into the kitchen when we did!

The three of us stood in the doorway watching helplessly as the black smoke continued to pour out of the broken pipe, covering the chairs, rug, curtains and ceiling with a thick film. It didn't take a genius to know that everything was ruined and would have to be replaced.

The next four days or so found me on my hands and knees scrubbing away the soot and clearing out all the irreparably damaged furniture. *What can all this mean?* I asked myself. *Surely God must be in this too.*

Because of the New Year, the Japanese were out in full force celebrating the holiday. For several days, everywhere I looked, excited children, along with women dressed in beautiful silk kimonos, roamed the streets calling on homes. It was a colorful sight, a stark contrast to me, covered in soot from head to toe, looking like a chimney sweep.

On the third day, as I was scrubbing away at the seemingly endless soot, tears of frustration began to run down my cheeks. I lifted my heart to the Lord, trying to discern some purpose for this seeming setback. Suddenly, unmistakably, I heard a voice say, "To humble you and prove you, to know what is in your heart. For this is what the high and lofty One says—he who lives forever, whose name is holy: 'I live in a high and holy place, but also with him who is contrite and lowly in spirit, to revive the spirit of the lowly and to revive the heart of the contrite.' "

The words came from Isaiah 57:15. It was clear to me that God was laying the foundations for a fruitful ministry, preparing my heart for what lay ahead.

Even with all the great things that were happening in Matsue and the surrounding area, when my furlough arrived I was anxious to go back to Canada. Some of my family had been involved in a car accident. Although no one was seriously injured, this near tragedy reminded me of just how far away from home I really was. I also discovered that my younger sister Betty had been spending a great deal of time taking care of Mother and was looking forward to some help.

I left Japan May 2, 1971, hoping and praying, as in previous years, for true revival to break out in the country I loved and had adopted as my own.

18

Paid in Full

Although my furlough year was exciting in some respects, it was also very difficult. What made it so were two rather significant events.

The first one took place during my fall missionary tour in and around Saskatoon, Saskatchewan. Revival broke out! It was incredibly exciting! On many occasions services lasted well into the night as the Holy Spirit moved in hundreds of lives. The revival also brought to light a heart-wrenching reality—a great many people were in need of deliverance from demonic oppression. I felt a tremendous burden to assist these people and I also saw it as an opportunity to gain valuable experience for future ministry in Japan.

Then, Mother suddenly suffered a heart attack and died. Although I had always sensed that she would die when I was on furlough, it still left me in shock. I knew she was with the Lord, but the thought of not seeing her anymore created within me an incredible emptiness.

However, over time God allowed the ache in my heart to subside as I witnessed many changed lives from the revival. In fact, having witnessed God's intervention in my home city, it made me yearn more than ever for a fresh moving of God's Spirit in Japan.

Returning in April of 1972, I received word that my new station would be in the city of Nagoya, the fourth largest metropolis in Japan with over 2 million inhabitants. Because my apartment was not immediately available, I became an itinerant preacher, moving from church to church, sharing the wonderful things that had happened in Saskatoon. I also made my way back to Matsue one last time to oversee the moving of my belongings.

Part of Japan's main industrial belt, the city of Nagoya led its prefecture in becoming one of the major industrial centers in Japan. Nagoya Castle, damaged extensively in the war and rebuilt in 1959, became the city's chief tourist attraction. The area also boasted various educational institutions including Nagoya University. As I was about to discover, these institutions would play a major role in the birthing of a church in this city.

My new residence was located in one of the

compounds owned by the Mitsubishi company, adjacent to a busy thoroughfare. Across the street was a row of large homes. Constructed after the war, they had been built for foreigners coming to help jumpstart the company. Employees from both McDonnell Douglas and Lockheed lived in those luxurious quarters. In comparison, the houses on my side of the road were much more modest, although more than adequate.

Besides the residential area, there were a number of universities in close proximity to my street, at least four within a five-minute drive, of which two actually bordered our compound. One university specialized in foreign languages. The other was the largest university in Nagoya. Many students walked by my place on their way to catch public transit.

When my belongings finally arrived, fellow missionaries helped me move the larger items into the house. Unfortunately, they couldn't stay long, so I took them to the train station. By the time I got back, it was already noon.

As I surveyed the threatening clouds above and the many boxes and containers that still cluttered the front yard, I knew there was no time to rest. So for the next three hours I transported box after box one at a time into the appropriate rooms.

When 3 o'clock rolled around, there was still much to do and the clouds were becoming even more menacing.

"Lord," I said, "let me just get all this stuff inside before it pours."

"Can we help?" a voice asked as I bent down to pick up another container. Looking up, I saw three girls.

"Oh, you three are angels!" I exclaimed.

"We're so glad you think so," one of them replied jovially. And with that, they put down their bags and pitched in.

We opened all the sliding doors on the street side and made countless trips to the house, always keeping an eye on the clouds. By 5, the last box was finally in one of the now cluttered rooms. No sooner had we stepped inside than it began to pour. *Thank You, Lord,* I prayed silently.

I managed to find a few chairs and offered the girls a seat. I didn't have anything to eat, but I was able to locate some coffee, a few cups and the coffeemaker. While I busied myself around the kitchen, I found out that my three helpers attended a girls' high school in the area and had been on their way to a transit stop.

As the luscious smell of the perking coffee began to waft throughout the room, I breathed it in deeply, anticipating how good it was going to taste. With the cups full, I sat down across from my "angels."

"Why are you here?" one of them inquired.

"To start a church," I replied.

"Where is your church building?" another asked.

"Well, I don't have one yet, but for the time being I'll be having it right here in the house." I glanced at the clutter around me and let out a big sigh.

"Well, when will you start services?"

I looked at the girl who had asked the question. Without thinking I told her it would be on Sunday.

"Tomorrow is Sunday," one of them said. "Can we come?" I had forgotten that today was Saturday!

I laughed at the thought of having a service in the midst of all the mess. However, I knew I was not about to allow any opportunity to pass me by, especially since they seemed to be genuinely interested.

"If you come, girls, there will be a service," I promised. With that I bid them goodbye. I feverishly began to make some room, working virtually the entire night to make the house presentable in the hopes that they would come back. I don't know whether I really expected them to show up or not. But when Sunday arrived, there they were at my doorstep. I found out later that it was no easy task for them to get there. Each one of them lived at least an hour away in different directions by subway.

I led the girls in a few songs and then gave them a short message. At the conclusion, they said they would be back the following Sunday. True to their word, a week later they were once again at my front door, this time each with a friend. By the end of the year, three of those young girls had accepted Christ. My work in Nagoya had begun.

With university students passing by my front door everyday, it occurred to me that there might be an easy way to expand my ministry. I decided to offer English classes. It had been successful in every other location, so why not here as well? In fact, this seemed the perfect place to do it.

Within days, one of the students constructed a couple of signs for my front yard: "Let's study the Bible while we study English," with my name neatly at the bottom. This made it obvious that they would be learning from a foreigner. In no time at all I was holding two classes a week and, by the beginning of September, two more young people had come to know Jesus as their Savior.

In the weeks and months that followed, I began a Sunday school for children and also launched a visitation program in the immediate vicinity. Initially there was little response, but that soon changed.

The second time around, one neighbor told me that the hymn singing she heard coming from my house had given her the impression that God had arrived. Just before Christmas, she began attending our church and shortly thereafter came to know Christ. It wasn't long before her son and daughter were also saved. Even her husband sat in on one of our services that first year.

Although having some early success in this neighborhood, I had doubts about whether or not this was actually the right place to start a church. The transient nature of the area, the large foreign population and the lack of available buildings with reasonable rental rates all led to my uncertainty.

After some initial leg work, I finally decided on an area called New Town, one of many satellite cities surrounding Nagoya, about a thirty-minute drive from the heart of the main city. It was composed of approximately 700 large apartment complexes, along with other residences which provided housing for hundreds of thousands of people. I also discovered that there was very little in the way of evangelism being done among them. *Surely this must be the place that God would have me be,* I thought. *After all, it's a complete city of Japanese people, with little or no outside influence.*

I spoke to the Mission director about my proposed plans for New Town. After looking things over, he agreed that we should relocate. It wasn't long before I found some suitable land and contacted a broker. The director arrived from Hiroshima to look over the property as well. He indicated that the Mission would try to raise the funds. Elated by the news, I asked God to send the money so that we could begin as quickly as possible. Some of the locals had already come to know Christ as their Savior, so needless to say I was very anxious to begin work there full-time.

However, as right as all this seemed to be, there was a nagging hesitancy within me that I found confusing. So I continued to pray. If I was to go to this new location, I wanted to be sure.

Within a short while I had my answer. God said no! I was astounded! But, there was no mistake. As perfect as everything seemed in New Town, I clearly heard God say "no," not in an audible voice, but just as clearly as if it had been. *I don't want you to go there, Susan,* He told me. *I brought you here to Nagoya. It's here that I will give you a church.* I had learned the hard way that to go against God's direction meant settling for second best. So even though I couldn't understand it, I threw all my energy into Nagoya, trusting that somehow God would take care of New Town.

The days and weeks went by with no apparent break in finding property near my home. I became increasingly impatient. Finally, in desperation I called out to God. "Lord, You told me You were going to give me a church in this area. Well, where is it?"

Several weeks later, during one of my prayer times, I suddenly had the distinct impression that I was to walk down my street toward the university on the hill. Rounding the corner at the base of the hill, I noticed two empty pieces of land, one on either side of the street. I shrugged. Having walked by those vacant lots many times, I had never really considered them to have potential. *Is this what God has in mind?* I wondered almost aloud.

The one on my side of the street was a small piece of land owned by the Mitsubishi company. On the far side were two larger lots. I had heard that they belonged to a company president and his wife who were hoping to build a large home there. I assumed that if these were my only choices, the smaller piece of property must be the one God intended for us to have, especially since it appeared that the Mitsubishi company had no apparent plans for it.

In the days that followed I wrote many letters to the company, but received no reply. Finally one day, a letter appeared in the mail. With my hands shaking, I tore it open. My excitement though soon changed to disappointment—they had other plans for the property and would not be selling it.

With an extremely heavy heart, I trudged down the street toward the empty lot, all the while wondering what God was trying to tell me. *I must have missed something,* I thought to myself. Arriving at the spot, I gazed longingly at the land one last time. Suddenly, something out of the ordinary caught my attention on the other side of the road—a "For Sale" sign! The two lots owned by the company president were for sale!

With three years having already elapsed since I first arrived in Nagoya, I wanted to get the funds right away and purchase the land immediately. But of course that was impossible. Instead, over the next number of months numerous contacts were made both with the owners and their broker.

We also contacted the Alliance headquarters in New York asking them for the funds to make the purchase. A few weeks later word came back from New York: They were thrilled with the opportunity to buy land in the area, but we would have to wait until the end of the fiscal year.

While I waited I poured my heart and soul into the work. My sister Betty arrived from Saskatchewan and worked with me for a year teaching at the girls' high school. We had a wonderful time serving God together. We also welcomed Dick and Eleanor Pease to our team and moved the church from my house to theirs. This provided us with much more space. Their leadership abilities and musical talent reaped almost instant dividends. Eleanor organized an orchestra and choir. It was a great attraction to the young people. The choir also performed at our ladies' Christmas luncheon attended by 355 women, nineteen of whom made decisions for Christ.

Early in December, word reached us that
New York had no money available. I was very
disappointed! After informing all the parties involved that the deal had come to a standstill, I
went to bed that night with mixed emotions.
Part of me was resigned to the fact that it was
over, yet I couldn't help but think that God
had other plans.

Suddenly awakened around 3:30 that morning,
I felt a strong urge to open my Bible. The first
words I came upon were, "The LORD has chosen
you to build a temple as a sanctuary. Be strong
and do the work" (1 Chronicles 28:10). With
those words of encouragement echoing in my
mind, I went to bed, thinking that maybe, just
maybe, God wanted us to step out in faith.

A day or so later I was somewhat surprised to
discover that the broker for the property owners wanted to see me. After the initial pleasantries were out of the way, he asked, "Did your
headquarters actually say that you couldn't
build?"

"No, they didn't say that," I replied, somewhat puzzled at the question. "They said they
had no money to give us."

He smiled.

"You have prayed so long for this, Susan. I
doubt if we could sell it to anyone else even if
we tried. I want you to know that the owners
are still very favorable to you and would very
much like to sell it to you as long as your headquarters is not opposed to it."

I could hardly believe what I was hearing! *Could it actually be that God still desired for us to have this land?* I hardly dared believe it!

The broker continued.

"I informed my clients of your financial situation. They have assured me you would not have to put any money down. In fact, they are willing to put up a pre-fab building which you can use any way you see fit. You won't have to pay anything until after you return from your furlough." I knew that Japanese law stated that any property sold without a building on it was subject to a fifty-two-percent tax. The pre-fab building would benefit both parties by providing the current owners with a huge tax break and our church with a temporary meeting place and a small apartment for two of our students.

"But this isn't really a good deal for your clients. What if you get a buyer who is able to give you cash for the land?"

"Well," he assured me, "we won't sell to them. My clients want to sell to you."

"I don't think it's fair not to pay you something," I insisted.

"Well then, if you want to pay something," he countered, after a moment's thought, "why don't you pay the amount necessary to complete the contract?"

A few days later our missionary team gathered together to pray about the offer. While we were all assembled, without warning, there came a knock at our door. There stood the brokers who had been involved in negotiating the deal. With them was the wife of the man who owned the property.

"I have a daughter attending university," she said. "She is a Christian. When I discovered that Susan was a missionary, I spoke to my husband about this land. We have decided we want you to have the property regardless of when you are able to pay for it. The only thing I regret," she continued, "is that I will not be here to attend your church."

After they left, we went to prayer once again. Finally, after much discussion, we agreed to the deal. When Mr. Kerr arrived from New York shortly after the New Year, I met with him before signing the contract. I read him an excerpt from a letter I had received from one of the faithful prayer warriors back in Saskatoon. "Remember, Susan, God isn't dependent upon New York."

"That's right, Susan, He isn't," Mr. Kerr responded with a smile.

What a day of celebration it was when we turned over $14,000 as an initial payment and received the deed to the property. It had taken four years, but God had provided even against what seemed like insurmountable odds.

Three-and-a-half years later, in June of '79, after much prayer and hard work, the building was finally up and the final payment had been made. What a joy it was to see the words "Paid in Full" stamped on the contract.

19

Rescued from Suicide

One of the dearest women I ever met was Mrs. Kobayashi. Reared like a princess in Japanese high-class society, she later married the oldest son of a company president who also happened to be a Buddhist temple priest.

I first saw Mrs. Kobayashi during my second Christmas in Nagoya. I was running a Sunday school for children out of my home. When it came time for the Christmas program, we sent invitations home with all the children, inviting the mothers to attend. One of the students was six-year-old Miwachan, Mrs. Kobayashi's daughter. She appeared to be a very nervous little girl and I wondered what could be troubling her.

Just as the program was about to commence, an elegantly dressed woman walked in and seated herself near the front. It was Mrs. Kobayashi. She caught my eye almost immediately because she was not dressed as the other ladies were—in western clothes. Instead, she wore a beautiful Japanese kimono and had her hair done up in the traditional style.

As the program progressed I kept glancing in her direction, puzzled by the lack of expression on her face. Even when our speaker had everyone either laughing or crying as she shared her testimony, Mrs. Kobayashi neither laughed nor cried. Her face masked all emotion, giving one the impression that she was virtually dead inside.

When the program ended, I stood and addressed the ladies.

"Tomorrow is the 26th of December, the last Christmas program of the year," I began. "It is just for you ladies. I'm going to put on a typical Christmas party with refreshments and goodies. Mrs. Masuda will again be our speaker. Please come. You're all invited back."

The next day the same ladies plus a few others, including Mrs. Kobayashi, were at my house. But once again she sat with that same expressionless look on her face. I couldn't help wondering what deep hurt was hiding there.

Mrs. Masuda's story focused on the years of intense suffering she endured in a Siberian prison. After concluding her impassioned speech, she sang a song about Christ's suffering on the cross. Just as she finished, one of the women in the audience threw herself forward, crumpling to the floor. Crying out in agony, she wailed, "I have despaired of life. Can this Jesus save me?" It was Mrs. Kobayashi! Gone was the carved rigidity of her countenance. Now I was looking at a broken woman whose pain was finally making its way to the surface. A few of us comforted her as best we could.

Although she made no decision to follow Jesus that day, I let her know I was there for her if she ever wanted to talk. Before the women left, I informed them that I would be going away for a few days but invited them to come and see me when I got back.

Returning several days later, no sooner had I opened my front door than the phone rang. It was Mrs. Kobayashi. She wanted to see me. Within five minutes a pleasant looking Japanese lady in western clothes was standing at my door.

"Hello. May I help you?" I asked courteously.

"Hello, Miss Dyck," came the reply, "I'm so glad you're back from your trip."

Puzzled, I smiled sheepishly.

"I'm sorry. I don't know who you are."

"I am Mrs. Kobayashi."

It couldn't be! This didn't look at all like the Japanese woman I had met a few days earlier. I commented on her North American dress, the new hair style, her upbeat spirit.

"I know," she responded. "I don't even recognize myself. It is my face, is it not?"

"Oh, yes," I replied. "You look like a new person."

"Miss Dyck. May I tell you my story?" she finally asked.

"Please do," I replied, hardly able to wait to hear the before and after account.

For years, she said, she had suffered humiliation from her in-laws, specifically her husband's older sister. It all began when her father-in-law arranged to turn over control of the factory to his oldest son, her husband. However, the eldest daughter plotted against her brother and finally persuaded their father to secretly take back control of the business.

What followed was eight years of bitter infighting among family members. Tension between Mr. and Mrs. Kobayashi grew as they constantly argued about the family's problems. Finally, with the laughter gone from the home and her despair mounting, Mrs. Kobayashi began to contemplate suicide. Since the option of leaving her husband would, according to Japanese custom, reflect poorly on him, suicide seemed the only alternative.

Some time later, their daughter Miwachan heard her parents arguing one night and realized that something was awfully wrong. The next morning she approached her mother.

"Mommy, don't be sad," she began. "If you want to separate from Daddy, it is alright. If you want me to be with you, I'll do that. But if you want me to stay with Daddy, I'll go with him."

It was shortly after that heart-wrenching incident that Mrs. Kobayashi decided to end her own life. In her state of mind, it seemed the only way out of her predicament. Methodically, she began to study the various ways to accomplish the grisly task. After eliminating several options, she finally decided to check out the high-rise buildings. Early one morning she found herself standing at the bottom of one of these magnificent structures. Carefully she studied the best location to jump from so that she could end her suffering once and for all. With the "perfect" spot chosen, she determined to do it later that day.

Japanese custom dictated that before a suicide attempt, a woman's house had to be spotless. She rushed home and feverishly set about the task, scouring every corner, making sure every drawer and closet was neat and tidy. Then she sat down to await the arrival of her little girl from school.

When Miwachan appeared, her mother calmly picked up the shopping basket.

"Mommy is going down to the store to shop for dinner," she said calmly. For Miwachan, this was nothing unusual. She often stayed home and played while her mother shopped for the evening meal. For some reason though, on this occasion, Miwachan reacted differently. Instead of happily running off to play, a look of fear came over her and she dashed to her mother. Wrapping her little arms around her mother's hips, she squeezed tightly.

"Mommy, don't die! Mommy, don't die!" she cried out, repeating the mournful words over and over again.

How could my daughter know? Mrs. Kobayashi wondered. *Could it be that there actually is a God?* That was the only thing that could remotely explain her daughter's action. How else could Miwachan sense that she was about to commit suicide? *Certainly this must be the voice of God,* she reasoned.

While she continued to mull this over, Miwachan became increasingly more clingy, imploring her mother not to die. Finally, Mrs. Kobayashi promised her daughter that she wouldn't take her life, and the child released her grip. Mrs. Kobayashi kept her promise and in so doing resigned herself to her fate. The family situation remained unchanged.

Then, one day, during the Christmas season, Miwachan arrived home from Sunday school where she had been with her playmates. She handed her mother an invitation to a Christmas program. With nothing else to do, Mrs. Kobayashi decided to go and show support for her daughter. That's where we first met.

I thought about her story for a moment, reflecting on the day she broke down in tears, remembering her desperate cry, "Can Jesus save me?"

"Mrs. Kobayashi," I said finally, "let's go back

to the song that Mrs. Masuda sang, the one that touched you so deeply, the one that spoke about Christ's sufferings." She nodded her head.

I went on to explain that no one ever suffered to the extent that Jesus suffered. I told her how He had been beaten, mocked and spit upon; how He had been cruelly nailed to the cross to die for the sins of mankind.

"Mrs. Kobayashi," I continued, "do you know what Jesus' first words were on the cross?" She shook her head. "His first words were, 'Father, forgive them for they know not what they do.' "

I paused, waiting for a response. Her eyes appeared vacant, as if she were staring beyond me. Then suddenly, she put her head on the table and began to sob uncontrollably, her tears forming tiny puddles on the kitchen table. I knew she had finally come face-to-face with Jesus.

After a while, she lifted her head and looked at me.

"I'll forgive her," she said. "I'll forgive my sister-in-law."

That day Mrs. Kobayashi accepted Jesus as her Savior and received complete freedom not only from her sin but from her despair. As she left, an unbelievable happiness surrounded her. That night she told her husband what Jesus had done for her. Her words had a profound effect on him and over the weeks that followed their marriage was restored.

A year later we decided to hold a baptismal service. Mrs. Kobayashi went home to ask her husband about it. Being from a Buddhist priestly line, Mr. Kobayashi's response was not at all certain to be affirming. So she was somewhat startled when he said, "Then be baptized."

"But what about your father, the priest?" she asked.

"Never mind him," came the reply.

Mrs. Kobayashi was baptized and later had an opportunity to tell her father-in-law and other family members about her newfound joy in Christ. The old priest responded with these words: "Oh, the power in religion and also in Jesus Christ." The father also moved in with the Kobayashis for a time. What was so miraculous about this was that he had never directly spoken to his daughter-in-law in all the years she had been married to his son.

A year or so later, the elderly Kobayashi was diagnosed with cancer. Mrs. Kobayashi faithfully cared for him until the day he died. As far as we know, he accepted Christ on his deathbed. Before he died, the estate problems were taken care of and family relationships restored.

Then, in July of 1979, Mrs. Kobayashi became very ill and I cried out to God once again for the gift of healing. One day in October, during the middle of the night, as I paced back and forth, my hands lifted up, imploring God to heal her, I heard God's voice speak to me very clearly: "This sickness is not unto death but to the glory of the Lord. It is done!"

The next morning I phoned Mrs. Kobayashi and informed her that she was healed! Puzzled by my words, she told me that the symptoms were still there. With what I can attribute only to the confidence of God, I responded, "Don't look at the symptoms. They will disappear."

Well, they did. She was miraculously healed, returned to church, headed up our ladies group and became one of the first board members of our church.

Although there were many other wonderful things that happened during those two terms in Nagoya, it was also during this time that I had to say goodbye to two dear friends whom God chose to take home.

One was Mabel Francis, my mentor and friend. It was a terribly sad day for me when she passed on to be with Jesus. But oh, the wonderful memories I had of this incredible woman of God. Her example to me of how to be a missionary had been indelibly imprinted on my soul.

The other friend was my dear old Japanese companion from Matsue, Mr. Kodake. Knowing that he was very sick, I went to visit him and we had a wonderful talk. He shared with me how God had continued to work in his life ever since the day he first accepted Christ as His Savior. Then he took my hand and wept.

Amidst the tears he said, "Miss Dyck, you gave me the new birth. Thank you!"

The following two days, Mr. Kodake underwent two operations. He died within a few hours of the second surgery. It was sad to see him go, but my heart was also glad. I had responded to God's call so that the people of Japan would hear about Jesus. Kodake was one of many who had not only heard, but responded.

20

God's Finishing Touch

During my thirty-two years on the mission field, I had the wonderful privilege of laboring together with some of the finest missionaries in the Alliance and various Japanese friends and colleagues. I was given many opportunities to win people to Jesus Christ and experienced a tremendous sense of fulfillment in bearing these spiritual children.

I had also battled against the forces of sin and darkness on behalf of others—and won. But those years were not without struggles of my own. Being a single missionary, there were times when I felt terribly alone, longing desperately for a husband and children of my own to care for. Eventually, deep inside a tunnel of despair from which I could perceive no way out, I felt totally inadequate for ministry. I should have seen it coming, but I didn't. It all came to a head my second year in Shobara.

Living in a mountainous region of inland Japan, I encountered many dangerous situations on the treacherous roads. One particular night, while commuting back from one of the remote stations, I had a rather harrowing experience. The slippery roads were even more precarious because only two tires on my vehicle were equipped with chains. So I made arrangements to travel in tandem with a friend following close behind.

Our journey began at dusk. As we slowly made our way along the narrow, winding road, my companion, forced by the road conditions, gradually pulled ahead of me. As he did so, the icy fingers of loneliness and fear began to clutch at my heart, heightening the tension I already felt. I glanced out the side window and over the edge of the road. There was only nothingness below. Added to my growing fear was the intermittent oncoming traffic whose headlights suddenly appeared out of nowhere, temporarily blinding me. When they eventually drew even with my vehicle, I felt as though I could literally reach out and touch them. Each time this scenario played itself out I gripped the wheel tighter and tighter, my anxiety increasing with every passing moment.

To make matters worse, at some point during this grueling ordeal, a truck traveling in the same direction as I careened passed me. Not too long after, I watched as he suddenly hit an icy spot, lost control of his vehicle and plunged into the chasm. There was nothing I could do for him, so I pushed on, praying diligently that God would get me safely through.

What should have been a one-and-a-half to two-hour trip became a five-hour struggle between me and the road, the steering wheel and my fears. When I finally pulled into my driveway, I was an emotional wreck. With a tremendous sense of relief, I dragged myself into the house, only to be met by yet another disappointment. The stove had gone out during my absence. The house was freezing!

"Oh, Lord," I complained, "why should I have to come home to this cold house when I've been out serving You? And why don't I have someone to care for me? Lord, I need a husband."

No sooner had the words passed my lips than conviction gripped my heart and I recognized my complaining for what it was.

"Oh, Lord, please forgive me for this self-pity. I'm sorry."

A still, small voice responded in my heart, *Your self-pity has to die.*

Unable to heat any water for a bath, I crawled into bed, shivering and too exhausted to care. Thankfully, I had an electric blanket.

The next morning, I awakened, still tense from the previous night's ordeal, my hands still clenched as if gripping the steering wheel. Although able to perform my ministry, from that moment on I seemed to encounter one hardship after another, all of which only increased my despair and loneliness. Something dark and foreboding was building within me.

Then, before Christmas, another harrowing experience left me even weaker emotionally. It happened one Saturday. Pastor Shizu Matsuyama and myself found ourselves once again on the mountain roads, visiting three of our outstations. Because twelve university students whom I had led to the Lord were going to be baptized in Shobara the next day, it was necessary for us to return to the city later that same night. I did not want to miss that.

It was around midnight when we finally left the last station. Needless to say, because of past encounters on icy mountain roads, I was not looking forward to the return trip. My fears were not unfounded. Once again the roads were incredibly treacherous and, part way into our journey, we hit some deep snow and got stuck. With little traffic on the road that night and unable to expect any help from the elderly Shizu, I dragged myself out of the car, unlocked the trunk, removed a shovel and began to dig away the snow from around the car.

When I eventually finished the task, I climbed back into the vehicle, exhausted, my fingers cold as ice. I took off my gloves and blew into my hands until they began to tingle. Then, putting the car into first gear, I slowly let the clutch out and stepped on the gas. After a moment or so, the chains grabbed the snow and we were off once again.

Hours later, my nerves in tatters, I stopped to let Pastor Shizu off at the church. Unable to restrain myself any longer, I leaned my head against the steering wheel and broke into tears. Shizu came around to the driver's side door.

"Miss Dyck," she began, gently putting her arm on my shoulder, "should I have my grandson put the car away?"

"Oh, yes!" I stuttered, wiping the tears from my face. "Please do. I just can't drive any more!"

I crawled into bed that night totally overcome with fatigue. The next morning I awoke extremely tired, a slight tickle in my throat. I knew I should stay in bed, but I couldn't.

Throughout the baptismal service, try as I could, I was unable to concentrate on or even rejoice in the great things God was doing in the lives of the new converts. Many of the students publicly thanked me for befriending them and leading them to Christ, but I hardly heard what they were saying. I was in an emotional fog and the cold virus was beginning to get the better of me. What was a victorious service for everyone else became an agonizing blur for me.

In the days that followed, my nerves were continually on edge. To add to my discomfort, my cold grew progressively worse. It was obvious that I was in desperate need of a rest. I had already purchased a ticket to fly to Taiwan for a vacation. The plan was to drive to Hiroshima, take a ship to Okinawa Island, a 600-700 kilometer trip, and then catch a flight from there to Taiwan. However, my visa had not yet arrived from Okinawa. That only added to my frustration.

By the New Year there was still no sign of my visa. I finally determined that if it wasn't in the mail that day I would proceed to Hiroshima anyway, ill health and all. Evening came and no visa. So, throwing a few things together, I dragged my fevered body to the car and began the arduous mountain journey to Hiroshima.

It was dark before I got on the road but I was desperate and terribly despondent. Never had I felt this kind of loneliness before. I spent virtually the whole trip grumbling and complaining to my Father in heaven. I told Him how lonely I was, how sick and tired I was of being by myself. I informed Him in no uncertain terms that it wasn't fair that I had no husband and family. "After all, who will take care of me when I get old," I reflected bitterly. On and on it went until many hours later I pulled into the Mission station at Hiroshima, safe but still terribly discouraged and very angry with God.

The staff quickly got me to a bedroom. As I lay in the darkness of the room that night, the only thing I could think about was the fact that I had left my electric blanket in Shobara. I grumbled to God that it wasn't fair that everyone else had theirs and I was without mine. It seemed like a fitting end to a miserable day.

A few days later, when my visa was finally tracked down, I left for Taiwan. The weather was perfect there and I soon felt better physically. However, emotionally and spiritually I had a long way to go. That became very evident a few months later when I received word that my father had died. I wasn't surprised by the news. I knew about his earlier stroke and subsequent stay in the hospital. However, that didn't make my sense of loss any easier to bear. The only trouble was, I was too busy to mourn.

Several months later, Mom sent me a film of the funeral. Since I had been unable to attend, she thought it would help in my grieving process. She suggested that I not view it by myself because the sight of my father lying in the coffin might be too much for me.

When Pastor Matsuyama heard about it, she asked if I would be willing to show it in the evening service in conjunction with my sermon. Knowing that the Japanese have a great interest in elaborate funeral ceremonies and memorials, I agreed.

I decided to preview it Saturday night at the home of one of the girls from our church. Her father, a photographer, had a projector that fit the reel, but we were unable to get together until 11 p.m. Not knowing how I might react, I wasn't looking forward to the walk home that late at night. We watched the film together, stopping it from time to time as I explained the various customs to my hosts. It was midnight before I finally left for home.

My earlier apprehensions were well-founded. Walking across the darkened school grounds, the same loneliness and sense of abandonment engulfed me. I also began to dread the empty house that awaited me. The closer I got, the worse I felt.

After what seemed an eternity, I finally reached the front steps and made my way to the entrance. But when I tried to set foot in the house, I couldn't. It seemed like the vacant building would swallow me up. Numerous times I tried to go in, but was turned away each time by the curtain of darkness that surrounded my heart.

Almost at my wit's end and in dire need of someone to talk to, I suddenly remembered a Christian friend who lived nearby. She was a nurse. Without another thought, I hurried over to her place. When I arrived, I noticed lights on in the house. Tentatively, I knocked. Her husband greeted me at the door. One look at my face and he knew something was wrong. I mumbled an apology for bothering them. He assured me that his wife was about to get up to go to work and wouldn't mind the intrusion.

The two of us sat and talked for a while. I don't really remember all that was said, but it didn't really matter. I just needed someone to

be with at that moment, someone to encourage
me. By the time she left for work, I was ready
to face my empty house.

At home, I turned on the light and sat down.
I realized that my grief and loneliness were not
the only things I was struggling with. I was also
experiencing a deep spiritual battle within. It
was time to sit down with God and have a long
talk.

"I don't know what's going on, Lord," I cried,
"but whatever it is, I need to get over it. I just
can't take this any longer." I felt terribly
ashamed at my weakness and extremely em-
barrassed that people knew of my despair. To
make things even more frustrating, I knew God
could supply all my needs. I had experienced
the filling of the Holy Spirit in my life numerous times. But for some reason I seemed to be
in an emotional and spiritual pit, totally inadequate to meet life's daily demands. I knew that
if God didn't meet me in a new way, I couldn't
go on.

During the course of that night I recalled a
previous conversation with Miss Francis. We
had discussed what it meant to be filled with
the Holy Spirit and how A.B. Simpson, the
founder of The Christian and Missionary Alliance, had given himself to the Lord so fully and
completely.

At one point in the conversation Mabel said,
"Susan, there have been many times when the
Holy Spirit filled me with His presence and

gave me the strength and the gifts necessary for ministry. But one time I felt like I didn't have enough strength to carry on. So I determined to give myself to the Lord like our founder had and then trust that God would meet me."

Her voice rose in excitement as she continued.

"As I gave myself fully to God, Susan, as I gave Him total control, the Lord provided me with even more of the Holy Spirit's power than I could ever have imagined!"

She paused as if awaiting my response.

"Miss Francis, I'm sure I have done that," I said somewhat confidently. There had been many times when I too was aware of the Holy Spirit's presence in new and powerful ways.

She acknowledged my experiences and then responded by declaring that the event she was talking about was a far deeper experience than she had ever envisioned or encountered before. Even though I felt I had given total control of myself to God, out of respect for Mabel's wisdom, I decided I would once again open my heart to God's provision, searching His heart and His desire for my life as she had done.

For the next two days I fasted and prayed. Finally, on the third morning, I awoke feeling somewhat at rest. The panic, the frustration, the despair, the emotional trauma that I had been experiencing was replaced instead with an unexplainable peace. With renewed confidence, I knelt by a chair and continued to wait upon the Lord. I sensed more was to come, so I determined to remain there until I received a clear answer from Him.

Sometime between 3 and 4 in the afternoon I stopped praying. Glancing at my watch, I realized I would soon need to get ready for my English class. Forty high school students would be waiting for me and I didn't want to disappoint them.

When I arrived at the church, I took my place on the stage and began the class. We started by singing a few hymns from some English/Japanese song books. The first song was "How Great Thou Art." Halfway through, I began to feel a strange sensation. Something was happening to me, but I didn't know what it was.

Thinking that others might be watching, I glanced nervously about, but no one gave any indication that they were aware of anything unusual. Uncertain as to what I should do next, I joined with everyone else and began to sing heartily, "This is my wonderful story—Christ to my heart has come; Jesus, the King of glory, finds in my heart a home. . . ."

As we got to that last phrase, an explosion of wonderful emotions erupted within me. Wave after wave poured over me in a continuous stream, so much so that I felt that I would be unable to endure it. The words of Dr. Simpson's hymn took on a new and refreshing meaning.

I am so glad I received Him,
Jesus, my heart's dear King;
I who so often have grieved Him,
All to His feet would bring.
Christ in me, Christ in me,
Christ in me—Oh, wonderful story;
Christ in me, Christ in me,
Christ in me, the hope of glory.

"Oh, Lord," I cried out silently, "let me get through this class! Please! What I'm feeling right now is overwhelming!" It was like heaven had come down in all its glory and Jesus was standing there right next to me. I knew He had come to take control of the throne of my life as never before. At that moment everything was clear, clearer than at any other time in my life.

As I taught that afternoon, tears flowed freely. Finally concluding my lesson, I bolted from the church. I took every shortcut I could think of, even stumbling my way across a rice paddy on the way. At the house, I headed for the kitchen and collapsed into a chair, still overwhelmed with emotion.

This is what Miss Francis was talking about! I thought to myself. She had once said to me, "Susan, He only comes in and possesses as much as you yield to Him. If you have secret places in your life, He can't have control of those areas." It was obvious that whatever secret places I may have had were no longer hidden from His presence.

Around midnight, I tried to get some sleep, but the waves continued crashing in upon me like giant swells in the surf. By morning my pillow was sopping wet. I thought I had known God intimately before this. I thought I had experienced Him deeply. But this was something far more profound than I ever imagined possible. It was absolutely exhilarating!

Naturally, the emotion didn't last forever, but that didn't matter. It was replaced with a deeper maturity in Christ and a complete assurance that He was unmistakably inside. Many experiences in future years confirmed that.

One such event took place as I was on my way to a speaking engagement on an island near Osaka, a city of about 6 million people. At the train station thousands of people were scurrying back and forth. In order to exit the area I had to make my way across an overhead bridge which provided me with a great view of the crowds below. Halfway across I happened to glance down momentarily. Suddenly I found myself weeping for the countless millions of the world. God spoke to me very clearly and said, "I died for them and I want you to tell them." It was another confirmation that I was indeed in God's will.

By this time God had also settled in my mind the issue of being single. The tremendous experiences and the closer walk with Him that ensued caused my loneliness to dissipate. In its place, God gave me complete satisfaction. Although for a while I still thought marriage might be a future possibility, an incident several years later settled that issue once and for all.

It was a year before the end of my third term. I was traveling home from a nearby village when I spontaneously burst into song. Although I often sang when traveling, there was something significantly different about this occasion—I had no idea what language I was singing in! My heart told me it was a song of worship, a love song to Christ!

Once I began, I couldn't stop. In fact, I continued singing my heart out till about 3 in the morning. The sense of worship reverberating through me was so real, yet, at the same time, difficult to describe. All I could determine was that I was experiencing a deep devotion to God, something amazing, something great, something glorious!

In the days that followed, I wondered what it all meant. Then, not too long after, while traveling in the car again, I found myself singing the same tune—in English. "I'll walk alone with You by the way of Calvary, I'll wear the crown of thorns for You, I'll go with You through Gethsemane. . . ."

Having received the interpretation of this love song to Christ, I knew my search was over. No longer would I wait or long for a husband

and a family. I now knew that God wanted me to remain single so that I could fully serve Him. The last vestiges of loneliness were finally gone. God had called me to be single and in His goodness He gave me intense satisfaction in it.

There is a wonderful addendum to the story about the song God gave me. It happened years later at a large missionary conference. A missionary from India stood up and gave a stirring report about what God was doing in his country. He ended by saying that he would like to teach the congregation a song in one of the Indian dialects. It was the very song I had sung to God years earlier! Not only that, it was also in the same dialect!

God in His infinite love had put the finishing touches on my life and ministry on the mission field in a truly unforgettable way.

Epilogue

On May 3, 1982, Susan left for her sixth term in Japan. It was to be a new location, a suburb of Tokyo called Machida. She was excited about the possibilities and immediately threw herself into this new venture.

But God in His infinite wisdom had other plans. A year and a half into her term, she was forced to return to Canada because of an as yet undiagnosed health problem. Never a woman to admit defeat, in July of 1984 she again left for Japan, convinced that God would heal her. However, ten months later she returned to Canada once more, never again to see her beloved Japan. Her sister Betty explains what happened next.

"I will never forget the day Susan's physician gave me the results of the test—it was positive. The brain scan revealed that Susan had Alzheimer's disease. Terrible, hopeless darkness flooded over me. 'Why, God? Why did You allow this to happen to Your faithful servant?' I cried.

"As I contemplated the devastating potential

of this dreaded disease, I was plagued by two thoughts: how would I eventually be able to care for Susan, and could or would God in His mercy just take her home? Then one day, I came upon the words to a hymn that were exactly what I needed to see me through the initial stages of Susan's care:

> God moves in a mysterious way
> His wonders to perform;
> He plants His footsteps in the sea,
> And rides upon the storm.

"The darkness left me. I knew God was there! He proved it time and time again in the months that followed as Susan's condition deteriorated.

"Despite the low periods, her love for God never wavered. I'd often find her with her Bible open, praying. She loved the people she had served and prayed that there would be a mighty outpouring of God's Spirit upon Japan. She also prayed fervently for her pastor, her church and her family.

"When the time came that I could no longer care for her, God graciously provided a place at the Circle Drive Alliance Special Care Home in Saskatoon. I believe she felt that with so many people around her she was back in Japan. She would often follow the nurse to the bedside of sick people, place her hand on them and pray for them.

"Today, as I write, Susan is silently resting, unable to speak. Why God is allowing her to linger so long, I do not know. But I do know He is still with her. On a recent visit I quoted the familiar passage about the Lord coming in the air, First Thessalonians 4:16-17:

> For the Lord himself will come down from heaven, with a loud command, with the voice of the archangel and with the trumpet call of God, and the dead in Christ will rise first. After that, we who are still alive and are left will be caught up together with them in the clouds to meet the Lord in the air. And so we will be with the Lord forever.

" 'Susan,' I said, 'Jesus is coming again and then you'll have a new body. You'll see Him and all your loved ones and those you led to the Lord in Japan.'

"Suddenly, her face lit up. She smiled and tried to speak. For a moment it felt like I was standing in God's physical presence. What a hope we have! Hallelujah!"

There is but one thing Susan is waiting for—her coronation day! What a celebration there will be in heaven when she arrives and hears the words that every child of God longs to hear: "Well done, good and faithful servant. Welcome home!"